Year of Grace

A Daily Companion

Year of Grace

A Daily Companion

The Sacre Coeur Center
for Healing and Spirituality

Sheed & Ward

Franklin, Wisconsin

As an apostolate of the Priests of the Sacred Heart, a Catholic religious order, the mission of Sheed & Ward is to publish books of contemporary impact and enduring merit in Catholic Christian thought and action. The books published, however, reflect the opinions of their authors and are not meant to represent the official position of the Priests of the Sacred Heart.

1999

Sheed & Ward
7373 South Lovers Lane Road
Franklin, Wisconsin 53132
1-800-266-5564

Printed in the United States of America

Cover and interior design: GrafixStudio, Inc.

Library of Congress Cataloging-in-Publication Data

Year of grace: a daily companion / by the Sacre Coeur Center for
  Healing and Spirituality.
    p. cm.
  ISBN 1-58051-062-0 (pbk.)
    1. Catholic Church Prayer books and devotions—English. 2. Devotional
calendars—Catholic Church. I. Sacre Coeur Center for Healing and Spirituality.
BX2130 .Y43 1999
242'.2—dc21   99-35186
                                                           CIP

1 2 3 4 5 / 02 01 00 99

INTRODUCTION

This work is our invitation to you to travel with us along the gospel path of faith. The following reflections are offered in the hope that they will enhance each day of your journey and thereby enrich the Christian invitation to which you respond.

It may prove helpful to set aside five or ten minutes of your busy day to rest with the meditation, knowing that you will not be alone. As you go aside to recline at the feet of the Master, know that wherever you are and whatever your situation may be, we carry you in our feeble efforts to pray. We would ask you to bear us with you in your silent moments, so that together we might allow the Lord to accomplish within us something beautiful for himself.

As you journey through these pages may the Son of God, who is already being formed in you, draw you into a deeper hunger for him, and may he grow in you until he becomes your all. May the blessing of his peace be upon you and your loved ones.

And Mary kept all these things, reflecting on them in her heart. (Luke 2:19)

Background
There are echoes here to the Old Testament, of how Joseph's father "pondered" on the dreams that Joseph shared with him (see Genesis 37:11) and of how Daniel, even though he was terrified by his thoughts, "kept the matter to himself" (see Daniel 7:28). Some scholars would see in Mary the prototype of the good soil that bears fruit a hundredfold, having first internalized and pondered God's word.

Reflection
Within Mary the seed of God's word finds a perfect home. In chapter 4 of Mark's Gospel, we are told that there are three stages involved in becoming fertile ground for God's word. First, we must hear the word. This involves being exposed to it in whatever way this is possible. Second, we have to accept it without being selective. Third, we have to allow it to bear fruit as it transforms our lives.

To Think About
We must change in order to remain the same. (G. di Lampedusa)

Prayer
Lord, may your word be a light on my path during the coming year. Amen.

January

2

And this is the testimony of John. (John 1:19)

Background

As John's Gospel was the last one to be written, John presupposes that his readers are familiar with the character of John the Baptist and the content of his preaching. Consequently, John the Baptist is introduced rather suddenly, without too much of an introduction. John then sets about contrasting the teaching of John the Baptist with the teaching of Jesus.

Reflection

How often we hear people say: "I wouldn't have believed it but I saw it with my own eyes." There is nothing that can replace firsthand experience. For John the Baptist, the encounter with Jesus throws a new light on many things. It enables him to have a greater knowledge of Jesus and of himself. Jesus is the light of the world that helps us see others and ourselves more clearly and to feel more at ease about everything.

To Think About

All experience is an arch to build upon.
(H. B. Adams)

Prayer

Lord, that I may see thee more clearly and love thee more dearly. Amen.

"Now I have seen and testified ..." *(John 1:34)*

Background

The Fathers of the Church claimed that it was only with the eye of the mind and soul that one can see that Jesus is the Son of God. John, having been privileged to experience the theophany at the baptism of Jesus, is testifying to his conviction. He is convinced, beyond any shadow of a doubt, that Jesus is the Son of God.

Reflection

We are told that preachers should preach not because they have to say something, but because they have something to say! Like John, we testify when we have seen. More than ever, our world needs witnesses who are willing to testify to the power of Jesus Christ. No matter how great or how small our experience of Jesus may happen to be, we are called to speak of it both by word and action. It is our privilege, and nobody can do it in our place.

To Think About

How can I know that I am loved by a God whom I have never seen unless I experience his love through his followers whom I do see?

Prayer

Lord, may I be your worthy witness this day. Amen.

January

4

Then they opened their treasures and offered him gifts of gold, frankincense, and myrrh.
(Matthew 2:11)

Background

The gifts that the Magi offer have special significance. Gold is the gift given to royalty and foretells that Jesus is to be a King. Frankincense is usually associated with the role of a priest, one who offers sacrifice; it points to Jesus as the High Priest. Myrrh is used for anointing the body after death and signifies that Jesus is to die and be our Savior.

Reflection

No matter how small our talent may be, if we put it at the service of the Lord, he will make something beautiful of it. Time and again we may well ask what we have to offer to him or to others. With a few loaves of bread and a few fish, he is able to feed five thousand. Will he not be able to do even greater things with the gifts we offer him, no matter how small they may appear to be?

To Think About

God has placed me in the exact place that he wants me to bloom.

Prayer

Lord, show me the immense amount of goodness that I have to offer others. Amen.

"Repent for the kingdom of heaven is at hand."
(Matthew 4:17)

Background
The kingdom of heaven is what Jesus comes to establish. Although many of Jesus' contemporaries think that the Messiah will establish a territorial kingdom that will be free from Roman dominion and interference, the kingdom that Jesus comes to inaugurate is to be a kingdom where peace and love will flourish. The first step to bringing this about is repentance.

Reflection
A young girl had her hand jammed inside a precious vase. Her dad had made several attempts to wrench his daughter's hand loose but without success. Then, just as he was about to take her to the hospital, the father noticed that his daughter appeared to have her fist closed tightly. Opening his hand, he asked her to do likewise. "Oh no, Dad," she replied. "If I were to do that I would drop the penny!" To turn to God we must let go of sin.

To Think About
Is there something in my life that is preventing me from opening to God?

Prayer
Lord, like the morning dawn, let your kingdom come. Amen.

January

6

Then, taking the five loaves and two fish ... he said the blessing, broke the loaves, and gave them to his disciples to set before the people.... (Mark 6:41)

Background

This miracle appears to have made a profound impression on the disciples because it is recorded in all four of the Gospels. In reading the account, we find allusions to both the messianic banquet, which will be celebrated when the Messiah takes his place at the end time, and to the Eucharist, which has a similar structure.

Reflection

This action of Jesus depicts the Christian calling. We are "taken" when we are called into Jesus' service through baptism. He "blesses" us in many different ways with talents of one kind or another. Quite often we are then "broken," since God, who created everything out of nothing, sometimes reduces us to nothing before using us. Finally, we are "given" for others. This is the essence of the Christian calling: to be for others.

To Think About

Those who bring happiness to the lives of others cannot avoid it themselves.

Prayer

Lord, may I be your servant for others. Amen.

He got into the boat with them and the wind died down. (Mark 6:51)

Background

We know little about the precise details of this miracle. It takes place between 3 a.m. and 6 a.m. at a point where the lake is only about four miles wide. We do know that, because of its position and surrounding landscape, storms can whip up in the Sea of Galilee with little warning. We also know that Jesus joins his disciples and calm is restored.

Reflection

On the sea of life we often find ourselves caught in the eye of a storm. It is then, as it is for the disciples, that our faith leads us to cry out to God. Jesus speaks of himself as the good shepherd and promises that he will be with us to the end of time! Even though we may not understand what he is doing with our life, we must never doubt his providence. He will never lead us to a place where he does not want us to follow.

To Think About

Faith is an inalienable part of your make-up; not something which you have got hold of, but something which has got hold of you. (Ronald Knox)

Prayer

The Lord is my shepherd, there is nothing I shall want. Amen.

"He has sent me . . . to let the oppressed go free."
(Luke 4:18)

Background

By choosing to read this passage from Isaiah (see 61:1), Jesus is setting out the manifesto for his future ministry. The oppression he speaks of is oppression imposed by the influence of evil. In his commentary on Psalm 126, Saint John Chrysostom tells us: "Sin exerts a more severe tyranny, evil takes control and blinds those who lend it obedience; from this spiritual prison Jesus Christ rescued us."

Reflection

While he was a young man, Abraham Lincoln went to New Orleans. There he saw a slave market where families were being split apart and members sold separately. Turning to a companion he vowed: "If I ever get a chance, I'll hit this hard." We know just how well he did this. Those we are being called to free may be people within our own family who are carrying burdens too heavy and who are seeking nothing more than a sympathetic ear.

To Think About

When I forgive another, I not only set them free; I free myself.

Prayer

Lord, may I light a candle of hope within those whom you bring across my path. Amen.

. . . but he would withdraw to deserted places to pray. (Luke 5:16)

January

9

Background

In Luke's Gospel we frequently find Jesus heading away to pray alone. We see this especially when an important decision is pending or when he has to deal with an important situation. For example, before he chooses the Twelve (see Luke 6:12), he spends the night in prayer. Again we find him praying before teaching his disciples how to pray (see Luke 9:18). In this instance, he is about to meet with the Pharisees.

Reflection

Much has been written about the prayer of Jesus. One of the many things we know is that the recorded prayers of Jesus, with the exception of his prayer for his disciples (see John 17), are short. To him can be attributed the words of Shakespeare in *Henry V*: "Men of few words are the best men." Many spiritual writers would hold that the fewer the words in our time of prayer, the deeper the prayer.

To Think About

More things are wrought by prayer than this world dreams of. (A. Tennyson)

Prayer

May I strive to rest in you as you rest in me. Amen.

January

10

"He must increase; I must decrease." (John 3:30)

Background

These are the last recorded words of John the Baptist and, as such, become an epitaph that speaks of the magnitude of the man. Whereas most of us would be reluctant to move from the center of the stage, John the Baptist joyfully steps aside for Jesus. These words are also a summary of his work and the mission that he fulfills in being a part of salvation history.

Reflection

The present day has been called the age of the great "I." However, it is only by God's grace that we are instrumental in accomplishing any good that we do. It would be as futile for us to claim any glory for ourselves as it would be to claim that the moon's brightness is its own light rather than the reflection of the sun's light. Christians may be the light of the world, but it is Christ's light that shines within them—not their own!

To Think About

And the Devil did grin, for his darling sin is pride that apes humility. (S. T. Coleridge)

Prayer

Lord, surround me with your light. Amen.

"You are my beloved son; with you I am well pleased." (Luke 3:22)

Background
Jesus is about to embark on his life's mission. Before doing so he has to be sure that this is what his Father wants of him. The first part of the assurance he receives is from Psalm 2:7 and is a description of the messianic King. The later part is from Isaiah 42:1 and refers to the servant of the Lord who will be subjected to much suffering. Jesus here learns that he is called to be a King who will suffer.

Reflection
There's a line from a song in *Phantom of the Opera* that says: "Love changes everything." The most important thing for our survival is to know that we are loved and that we are loveable. We need to hear this message not just at head level; it needs to take the longest journey of all—the journey from the head to the heart. Fear sometimes changes lives; love always does.

To Think About
May the realization of your love for me melt my hardness of heart.

Prayer
My Father loves me. Amen.

He saw Simon and his brother Andrew ...they were fishermen. ... "Come after me ..." (Mark 1:16-17)

Background

When Jesus begins his mission, he sets about choosing some helpmates. It is rather interesting to note that he is not too concerned about their background; he calls them while they are going about their daily work, just as the Lord "took me (Amos) from following the flock" (Amos 7:15). In all probability, the people Jesus chooses as helpmates are drawn to him by his preaching; without a doubt, they also are drawn to him because of who he is.

Reflection

Give a violin to a concert violinist and he or she will make a different kind of music than the child who is just beginning to take violin lessons. In a master's hand, we expect results that are out of the ordinary. When Jesus calls us, he calls us as we are; what we become depends on how we give ourselves to the work that he allots to us. Of ourselves, we may feel that we are of little worth; if we work with God, we are invaluable.

To Think About

God has a special plan for me.

Prayer

Father, may I be aware of the difference I make. Amen.

. . . for he taught them as one having authority. . . .
(Mark 1:22)

Background
At the time of Jesus, a rabbi had the authority to impose a decision that was binding. This, however, is not the authority that is given by Jesus. The Greek word for the authority that is attributed to Jesus is *exousia,* which means "the authority that belongs to the Messiah." It is the same authority that he uses to overthrow the rule of Satan.

Reflection
To be an outstanding teacher, three qualities are necessary. The teacher must love the pupils; the teacher must love the subject; and the teacher must have a thorough knowledge of what he or she is attempting to teach. Jesus is such a teacher. He comes to show us the Father's love. He experiences this to such an extent that he can claim that the Father and he are one (see John 10:30). He also has a profound love for those with whom he communicates.

To Think About
Christianity is caught not taught.

Prayer
Lord, may your love in me radiate to others. Amen.

January 14

Rising very early before dawn, he left and went off to a deserted place, where he prayed.
(Mark 1:35)

Background
Here we find Jesus praying at a time when he is under stress because the true nature of his miracles and his mission is being misunderstood. He also prays when his followers fail to comprehend the significance of the multiplication of the five loaves and two fish (see Mark 6:46) and when he is undergoing his agony in the garden (see Mark 14:32-42). When troubled, Jesus—like the rest of us—turns to his Father!

Reflection
There is always the danger that we can become so absorbed with the work of the Lord that we neglect the Lord of the work. If we are to do what God wants of us, we have to learn to be aware of him in the briefest moments of our lives. One of the fruits of prayer is prayerfulness, i.e., the ability to gently pull back the cloak that so often conceals the divine beneath the human.

To Think About
The world is charged with the grandeur of God. (G. M. Hopkins)

Prayer
May I see your gentle touch in each moment of my day. Amen.

"If you wish, you can make me clean." (Mark 1:40)

Background
Because leprosy is contagious, the Law declares that lepers are impure and that they contaminate the places and people with whom they come into contact. Leprosy is considered to be a punishment from God and, conversely, its disappearance is considered as one of the many blessings that the Messiah brings when he comes. This passage portrays Jesus listening to the earnest prayer of someone in need.

Reflection
Some people's understanding of prayer is a matter of trying to bend God's will to conform to theirs. But prayer is, essentially, our effort to get to know and do what God wants of us. The prayer of the leper, in this gospel passage, is a beautiful model of true prayer. There is probably nothing he wants more for himself than to be made clean, but he acknowledges that it must be Jesus' wish first.

To Think About
Often our service to God is as advisor.

Prayer
Not my will, but thine be done. Amen.

January

16

Unable to get near Jesus because of the crowd,
they opened up the roof above him. (Mark 2:4)

Background

The roofs of many Palestinian houses are normally
flat and act as a veranda where one can go for a bit
of privacy and peace. The roof consists of beams
that reach from one wall to another, about three feet
apart. The spaces between the beams are packed
with brushwood and clay. The roof is accessible by
steps at the back of the structure, and the earth
between the beams can easily be dug out.

Reflection

We are told that where there's a will there's a way.
While an ordinary person will go to certain lengths
to accomplish some feat, the extraordinary person
will not be dissuaded. With a little extra effort we
can be outstanding followers of Christ. What a pity
we're too often willing to settle for second best.

To Think About

You must work as if everything depended on you
and trust in God as if everything depended on Him.
(Saint Thérèse of Lisieux)

Prayer

Lord, may I be satisfied with nothing less than my
best. Amen.

"Those who are well do not need a physician, but the sick do." (Mark 2:17)

Background
The upright Jew has little more than contempt for the one who is wayward—the sinner! This contempt is made worse by the fear of contamination from associating with the person. For the upright Jew, to have anything to do with a sinner is anathema. Thus, in failing to accept their own sinfulness, upright Jews cannot be helped by Jesus. In fact, Jesus is for them what the proverbial red flag is for a bull.

Reflection
An old priest used to preach that the cross we bear in life is often our greatest blessing in disguise. If we don't have the experience of the cross in our lives, would we, in fact, experience our great need for Jesus? The greater our struggle to overcome sin, the more we can rest assured that Jesus has come for us. We are the lost sheep that he searches for.

To Think About
Therefore trust the physician, and drink his remedy in silence and tranquillity. (K.Gibran)

Prayer
May the cross I carry be yours. Amen.

January
18

"Fill the jars with water. Draw some out now and take it to the headwaiter." (John 2:7-8)

Background
Some scholars see a reference here to the opening chapter of Genesis (see Genesis 1:6ff), where order and beauty are brought out of a formless void of water. The headwaiter is the one whose responsibility it is to make sure that there are sufficient supplies and that everything goes as smoothly as possible. This is why the new wine is brought to him for his approval.

Reflection
Time and again in the New Testament we find Jesus turning the impossible into the possible. From a few loaves of bread and a few fish, he feeds thousands; with a simple command he exorcises people or becalms the elements; with a touch of the hand he restores sight. Provided we do what he tells us, Jesus can take the rather insipid water of our efforts and transform it into life-giving nourishment for others.

To Think About
The difficult is what takes a little time; the impossible is what takes a little longer. (F. Nansen)

Prayer
Lord, may you make for yourself something beautiful of my life. Amen.

"No one pours new wine into old wineskins."
(Mark 2:22)

Background
When wine is new, it ferments and needs room for expansion. The container used to hold the wine in Jesus' day is not a bottle but skins. When the wineskins are new and fresh, they have a certain amount of elasticity. When they become old, however, they are rigid and have little "give." Consequently, it is essential that new wine be stored in new skins.

Reflection
A newly converted Christian was being taunted by a non-believer who asked him how many disciples Jesus had. The man replied: "I do not know. I'm ashamed of how little I know about him. All I do know is that three years ago I was an alcoholic, my marriage was on the rocks, my wife and children were starving, and I was unemployable. I committed my life to Jesus and now I'm sober, there's enough food for us to eat, and I have a job."

To Think About
When Christ enters the heart, he changes us from the inside out.

Prayer
Lord, I am not worthy to have you within my life. Say but the word and I shall be healed. Amen.

January

20

"Why are they doing what is unlawful on the sabbath?" (Mark 2:24)

Background

The Sabbath observance is of prime importance to the Jew. Its observance is conditioned by the proverbial thousand and one rules—many of which are ridiculous. Any semblance of work is forbidden. Work is catalogued into nearly forty different types, three of which are reaping, threshing, and meal preparation. The disciples, by their simple action, are deemed to have broken all three!

Reflection

The saying: "You cannot judge a book by its cover" is one of the truest ever spoken. So often we see an incident and, putting together what appears to be "two and two," we get five—because we look with the eyes of the head instead of with the eyes of the heart. Only in genuinely loving others can we hope to understand what they are doing and where they are coming from.

To Think About

You see but do not observe. (Sir A. Conan Doyle)

Prayer

May loving be mine and judging thine. Amen.

"Is it lawful to do good on the sabbath rather than to do evil, to save life rather than to destroy it?" (Mark 3:4)

January

21

Background
At the time of Jesus, the Jewish observance of the Sabbath gets to a point where it becomes counter-productive. Good, such as healing, is forbidden because it is classed as "work." At most, an injury can be prevented from becoming worse but never can it be made better! So rigid is the interpretation of the Law that people even refuse to defend themselves on the Sabbath.

Reflection
Rules and laws are important; they enable any community to live in relative harmony. There can be times, however, when we need to examine our priorities to see if our rules are effective. The ultimate law, of course, is the law of love. As Saint Augustine said, "We can love God and do what we will." When love becomes the rudder in the boat of our lives, we can rest assured that we will be traveling in the right direction.

To Think About
If I act out of love, I need not fear judgment.

Prayer
Lord, you are my guiding light. Amen.

January

22

Those who had diseases were pressing upon him to touch him. (Mark 3:10)

Background

As Jesus' ministry grows, so does his popularity. The crowds that follow him increase to such an extent that the situation becomes dangerous—there is the danger that Jesus might be crushed by the mob. So great is the demand for him, in fact, that even the sick do not wait for him to touch them; instead, they hustle to touch him, realizing that healing goes out from him.

Reflection

A wit once remarked that he wanted to go to heaven for the comfort but to hell for the company! Being a sinner is a blessing in disguise because Jesus tells us that he did not come to call the righteous to repentance but the sinner. When we struggle to overcome sin and its effects, Jesus can do something for us; without the struggle, Jesus can quite easily become an optional extra.

To Think About

The struggle itself towards the heights is enough to fill a human heart. (A. Camus)

Prayer

Lord, be merciful to me a sinner. Amen.

He appointed twelve ... that they might be with him and he might send them forth to preach.
(Mark 3:14)

Background
The phrased "he appointed" is the same one used for the appointment of priests. Behind the appointing of the twelve apostles lies the notion that Jesus is appointing the twelve tribes of the new Israel. The Twelve are to be "with him," which is the phrase Mark uses to explain the meaning of Christian discipleship.

Reflection
While it may sound like a cliché, there is much truth in the little phrase that says, "We must learn to be with God for others before we can hope to be with others for God." Who will show us the beauty of another better than God? Who better to show us what is for another's benefit than God? Like the Twelve, we have to listen to him in prayer if we wish to speak of his love to others.

To Think About
When I feel powerless to help others, I can place them in God's hands—and they will be safe.

Prayer
Create within me, Lord, a listening heart. Amen.

January

24

He came home. (Mark 3:20)

Background

Jesus waives aside the stability of the family business, provokes the wrath of the religious leaders of his day, and starts a peculiar little group of his own. Small wonder his relatives and friends feel that he has taken leave of his senses. It is because of this that they decide to save him from his chosen path. Even Jesus' family and friends do not appreciate what he is about.

Reflection

"Home is where the heart is." It is the place or situation in which masks can be lowered and we can find the freedom to be ourselves, knowing that we are accepted for who and what we are. We have the opportunity to make home a heaven or a hell. In a sense, home is like a cup of coffee; it's all in the way we make it.

To Think About

Are others better off or worse off for my living where I do?

Prayer

May I keep my eyes focused on my true home. Amen.

"The Spirit of the Lord is upon me, because he has anointed me to bring glad tidings to the poor." (Luke 4:18a)

Background
This verse refers to the promise made in Isaiah 61:1-2, which is fulfilled when the Messiah comes. Jesus is telling his listeners that this prophecy is being fulfilled in him. However, it is only those who adopt a stance of openness before God—who are poor not just socially but in their disposition before God—who will be capable of receiving these glad tidings.

Reflection
Jesus comes into our world with a unique mission: to save us and to show us how a child of the Father should live. No one else can accomplish what Jesus does. This is similar to the vocation that we are given: We are in this world with a special message to deliver, with a special song to sing. No one else can speak our unique message or sing our unique song. That message, that song, has been entrusted to each of us individually.

To Think About
Happiness lies not in seeking more but in developing the capacity to enjoy less.

Prayer
Lord, may my inner happiness of knowing you shine forth to others. Amen.

"But no one can enter a strong man's house to plunder his property unless he first ties up the strong man." (Mark 3:27)

Background

Prior to the coming of Jesus, Satan's power holds sway. Jesus, as the stronger force, is the only one capable of upending the rule of Satan. With Jesus' coming, a new age dawns: the age of the kingdom of God in which we are privileged to live. Jesus himself tells us: "Now is the time of judgment on this world; now the ruler of this world will be driven out" (John 12:31).

Reflection

It is amusing to watch an adult and a child playing together. At some point, the adult may actually feign doing his or her utmost, thus allowing the child to "win." If the adult were to perform to his or her fullest abilities, of course, the child wouldn't stand a chance of winning. When we are living a life of union with Jesus, we are in a similar position: invincible!

To Think About

Happy are those who find refuge in you. (Psalm 84:6)

Prayer

Keep my footsteps firm in your ways. Amen.

And looking around at those seated in the circle he said, "Here are my mother and my brothers."
(Mark 3:34)

Background
Jesus is not disowning his mother or insulting her in any way. Rather, he is trying to emphasize that those who respond to his call to discipleship will enjoy an intimacy that supersedes the bonding forged by blood. The word *brothers* in Aramaic is a broad term used when referring to nephews, cousins, and other relatives.

Reflection
Albert Schweitzer was one of the greatest intellects of recent times. He earned doctorates in theology, philosophy, music, and medicine. He then went to Africa, where he "wasted" his talents living and working with humble people. When asked why he chose to do so, he simply replied: "I was obedient to Christ." To belong to Christ's family we must learn obedience. To learn obedience we have to listen to him.

To Think About
Jesus does not need admirers or advisers but adherents.

Prayer
Speak, Lord, your servant is listening. Amen.

January

28

"Some seed fell among thorns, and the thorns grew up and choked it and it produced no grain."
(Mark 4:7)

Background

The farmers in Palestine often top, or pinch off, the weeds rather than digging deep to uproot them. Because of the climate, the weeds grow with such speed that they choke anything that grows about them. Hence, the seed does not stand a chance. It is the same with life. Quite often the weeds of business take over our lives, leaving less time for Jesus.

Reflection

The thorns that prevent us from bearing fruit for Jesus will often be well hidden. Because of this we need to be scrupulously honest. Help in gaining this honesty can be found in the company of a guide or soul friend, someone who can help us take an objective look at our lives. Some may feel that they do not need a guide. Yet, it has been said that the person who has himself or herself for a guide is little more than a fool.

To Think About

There are none so blind as those who do not wish to see.

Prayer

Lord, may I be honest enough to acknowledge sin as sin. Amen.

"To the one who has, more will be given; from the one who has not, even what he has will be taken away." (Mark 4:25)

Background
We have to learn to walk before we can hope to run. Before we are capable of carrying a great load, we have to be capable of carrying a light one. Jesus is not just explaining a simple truth to his disciples; he is entrusting a priceless treasure to them—the "secret of the kingdom." As they grow in acceptance of his teaching, they will understand its deeper significance.

Reflection
A story is told of a tiny spider that was trapped inside a watch when it was closed. The spider did what all spiders do—it spun a web and thereby caused the workings of the watch to cease operating. Shortly afterwards, the watch was opened for repair and the spider escaped. By doing what it was best at doing, the spider saved its life! When we use the talents we know we have been given, we discover other talents that we never thought we had.

To Think About
If the heart is loyal, God can use you. It is really all a matter of heart. (D. L. Moody)

Prayer
Lord, help me understand that what matters is the love with which I live my life. Amen.

January 29

January

30

"Of its own accord the land yields fruit, first the blade, then the ear, then the full grain in the ear."
(Mark 4:28)

Background
Jesus tells us that the growth of the kingdom will take place in an imperceptible way. Even though it may be difficult to notice the growth, it will achieve results of which we may never have dreamed. The growth of the kingdom of God may be silent but it will take place; it will be a silent, unceasing process that nothing will be able to stop.

Reflection
Embroidery has been called the analogy of life. While each stitch may appear small and insignificant, it is only when the work is completed that its full beauty and significance can be seen. Our daily behavior is similar to embroidery; each act we perform is part of the overall pattern of life. It either enhances or destroys its beauty. If each act is undertaken with love and care, we weave our lives into something beautiful for God and others.

To Think About
The essential thing is not to have won but to have fought well. (Baron P. de Coubertin)

Prayer
Lord, may I live today as if it were my first and last. Amen.

Then he asked them, "Why are you terrified? Do you not yet have faith?" (Mark 4:40)

Background

Some scholars think that this comment was added by the Evangelist and was not something that Jesus said. When he wrote it, the Evangelist may have been thinking of how Jesus' disciples abandon him at the time of his death. The whole incident must be seen not as something that took place some two thousand years ago but rather, as something that takes place time and time again in our own lives.

Reflection

Francis de Sales used to advise his followers that they were to be like children and walk through life with one hand firmly holding God's hand. The other hand was free to handle the world's business and thereby ensure that they never became too preoccupied with things that were temporal. If God is our companion on our journey, we will not only keep things in proper perspective, but we will learn that we are never alone.

To Think About

Today is the tomorrow I worried about yesterday— and all is well!

Prayer

Lord, may I realize that you are always by my side. Amen.

February

1

. . . all spoke highly of him. . . . They rose up, drove him out of the town. . . . (Luke 4:22, 29)

Background

Something happens between these two events that causes the crowd to turn on Jesus. In his preaching, Jesus is saying that the Gentiles, whom the Jews regard as little more than trash, are especially dear to God. The Gentiles, in fact, are every bit as entitled to experience God at work as are the Jews, who think themselves not only chosen but above others.

Reflection

We are told that the one who marries popularity will be widowed in a short while. One sure way to lose popularity is to speak the truth for, as an old Hebrew proverb reminds us: "Truth is heavy and few therefore can bear it." Provided it is spoken in love, the truth will liberate us; the truth will set us free. To settle for less is to live enslaved to sin.

To Think About

Beauty is truth, truth beauty,
that is all ye know on earth,
and all ye need to know. (J. Keats)

Prayer

Lord, may I proclaim the truth with my tongue and with my life. Amen.

... they took him up to Jerusalem to present him to the Lord.... (Luke 2:22)

February

2

Background
From the Book of Numbers (see 18:6) we know that there was a ceremony for every firstborn male, called the Redemption of the Firstborn. This may have been a carryover from the time when child sacrifice was prevalent. It is more likely that it was a recognition of God's power in giving life. The ceremony normally took place a month after the child was born.

Reflection
It has been said that the only thing children wear out faster than their shoes are their parents! So often parents act as if their children are truly theirs, forgetting that every child, like every gift, is given to us on loan. Parents worry and fret about their children as if they are their "possessions." The greatest thing parents can do is to offer their children to the Father each day, asking him, the creator, to watch over and protect them.

To Think About
Your children are not your children. (K. Gibran)

Prayer
Lord, I thank you for all that you have given and place it under your divine protection. Amen.

February
3

... [he] said that she should be given something to eat. (Mark 5:43)

Background
Mark views the incident of the raising of the young girl as a raising from the dead. What Jesus declares in this incident is that death is only a form of sleep from which one is awakened; it is not an end. When Jesus tells the little girl to "arise," the verb used is *anistemi,* which is the same verb used in the Scriptures when referring to Jesus' own resurrection.

Reflection
When Jesus encounters people, he touches them at practical, emotional, and spiritual levels; he is concerned with the whole person. If we hope to bring Jesus to people, we must do so in a way that deals with the person as a whole. Before we can preach the gospel in words, we must preach it by our actions. It is difficult to listen to the gospel on an empty stomach!

To Think About
How can I expect people to believe in God if they do not first see God in my actions of love?

Prayer
Lord, give me a loving, generous heart. Amen.

"A prophet is not without honor except in his native place...." (Mark 6:4)

Background
The Coptic "Gospel according to Thomas" gives a slight elaboration on this verse. It states: "No prophet is acceptable in his own village; no physician cures those who know him." It is very much the question of familiarity breeding prejudice and contempt. Because there is no acceptance of Jesus, the correct ambience for miracles to take place is not present and he is forced to move further afield.

Reflection
It has been said that there is nothing heavier than a child who does not want to be lifted. Similarly, there is nothing more difficult than to work in a situation where one is not welcome. How often do we deprive ourselves of a person's talents or friendship because of our refusal to accept that person. Judging others blinds us to their true beauty and thereby blinds us to the truth.

To Think About
Ignorance is less remote from truth than prejudice. (D. Didert)

Prayer
Lord, may I see your reflection in everyone I meet this day. Amen.

February

5

So they went off and preached repentance.
(Mark 6:12)

Background
The idea of being in need of repentance is difficult
for most of us to accept, because it implies that our
lives are not what they should be. Indeed, there
always is need for improvement. Repentance
involves a turning away from one way of life toward
another. This presupposes a change of heart, a
change in the way we view people and life. Only
when this change has occurred can we hope to
change the way in which we act.

Reflection
An old mystical saying tells us to "give up what thou
hast, then shalt thou receive." Repentance opens the
door to all kinds of new beginnings. It requires
being discontent with what we have, wanting to
bring about change, and taking the necessary steps
to bring about that change. Many of us want to enjoy
a closer walk with Jesus but we are not prepared to
take the necessary steps.

To Think About
How pleasant it is, at the end of the day, no follies to
have to repent. (A. J. Taylor)

Prayer
Teach me, Lord, to let go of what is, so that I may
enjoy what can be. Amen.

... for his fame became widespread ... (Mark 6:14)

Background

While residing in Galilee, Herod lives at Tiberias. This is predominantly a Gentile city and it is highly unlikely that Jesus goes there. Because of this, Herod does not have an opportunity to meet Jesus. The miracles that Jesus works, however, are reported far and near and, in this way, Herod may come to learn about him.

Reflection

Our desire to be famous is but an expression of our need to be accepted. But fame can rob us of our privacy and "ordinariness"; it can also bring unwanted pressures. To the extent that we make Jesus a partner in life, our craving for fame will diminish. He will become our all. What matters is not what others may think of us but what Jesus knows about us.

To Think About

Fame and tranquillity can never be bedfellows. (M. E. de Montaigne)

Prayer

Lord, may you remain constantly in my sights. Amen.

"Come away by yourselves to a deserted place and rest a while." (Mark 6:31)

Background
Mark suggests that Jesus invites his disciples to a deserted place for rest because of the hectic mission they've endured. The concept of "rest" is often used in connection with God as shepherd; the one who leads his flock aside to rest. This is portrayed in such scenes as Psalm 23:2 (the Shepherd Psalm), Ezekiel 34:15, and Isaiah 65:10.

Reflection
Life has been likened to a bottle of muddy water; as long as it is kept in motion, it is impossible to see anything but swirling particles of mud. Given time to rest, however, the mud settles and the water becomes clearer. Given time to rest, we gain a different perspective of ourselves and life in general. A life that is too busy for "time out" is merely a form of existing—not living.

To Think About
I am the master of my fate;
I am the captain of my soul. (A. W. D. Henley)

Prayer
Slow me down, Lord, so that I may see where I'm going. Amen.

... they left everything and followed him.
(*Luke 5:11*)

Background

Luke's Gospel has been called the Gospel of Renunciation. He is the only Evangelist to include the short phrase: "They left everything." This is all the more significant in the light of the tremendous catch of fish the apostles have just made. It's not enough that Jesus' disciples leave all they might possess. Leaving everything has to be done for a purpose—and the purpose must be to "follow" Jesus.

Reflection

A story is told of how Jesus, while walking along the edge of a cliff one day, heard piteous cries for help. Looking down the side of the cliff, he saw a man clinging to a branch. Jesus explained who he was and asked the man if he believed that Jesus could save him. "Oh! yes" replied the man, "I do believe." "O.K." said Jesus. "If you really believe, let go." "Is there anyone else up there?" asked the man! It is difficult to leave everything—even for Jesus' sake!

To Think About

The vocation of every man and woman is to serve other people. (L. Tolstoy)

Prayer

Lord, help me to trust in you. Amen.

February
9

. . . and as many as touched it were healed.
(Mark 6:56)

Background

This summary echoes the healing of the woman who has suffered with a hemorrhage for twelve years (see Mark 5:25ff). Those who practice alternative medicine, such as homeopathy, will claim that a remedy works because its electromagnetic field resonates with that of the person who is ill. Jesus, as the divine healer, emits an aura that is powerful.

Reflection

Expectant faith opens us to the possibility of miracles. Without it, miracles are reduced to mere coincidences. When we learn to see the imprint of God's hands on everything that happens each day, we come to appreciate how all of life is an extended miracle that gradually unfolds. It is then that we truly walk with God and live for him.

To Think About

The acts of our Maker ought always to be reverenced without examining, for they can never be unjust. (Pope Saint Gregory I)

Prayer

May my world be large enough to encompass you, and small enough for me to manage. Amen.

"Why do your disciples not follow the tradition of the elders but instead eat a meal with unclean hands?" (Mark 7:5)

February

10

Background

The "tradition of the elders" is as sacred and binding to the Pharisees as anything written in the Torah, or the Law. For example, there is a special way of washing the hands. Water is first poured over the tips of the fingers and is allowed to run up to the wrist. Then the palm of one hand is washed by rubbing the fist of the other into it. Finally, water is poured again, this time beginning at the wrist and running down to the fingertips.

Reflection

Traditions are important because they often enshrine both the sacred and the secular heritages of a family, group, or race. We must never be afraid to examine our traditions, however, or allow them to be examined by others. It is only when they are founded on love and when they promote love that they are worth preserving. Ultimately, very few things really matter in life.

To Think About

Tradition presupposes the reality of what endures. (I. Stravinsky)

Prayer

Lord, help me to examine the sanctity of my sacred cows. Amen.

February

11

"Nothing that enters one from outside can defile that person; but the things that come out from within are what defile." *(Mark 7:15)*

Background

With this statement Jesus lays aside the dietary laws for which many Jews have shed their blood and even given their lives. Jews today still have a list of foods that they consider to be clean or unclean. In a nutshell, Jesus tells his listeners that it is our actions that defile us, not anything we eat.

Reflection

Life is a series of choices. Through the choices we make, we become the person we want to be. A different life can begin for us right now but only if we choose such! The decision is ours and nobody else can make it for us—it's a decision that we must make for ourselves!

To Think About

I have set before you life and death ... Choose life. (Deuteronomy 30:19)

Prayer

Lord, may your Spirit guide me along the path of obedient service. Amen.

He entered a house and wanted no one to know about it. (Mark 7:24)

Background
At this period in Jesus' life, things are not going well. He has been rejected by his own people in Nazareth; Herod has come to regard him as a nuisance; and the scribes and Pharisees see him as an outcast who disregards many of their traditions and laws. Jesus, quite understandably, moves north from Galilee to Tyre, to allow time for the dust to settle and to recharge his batteries.

Reflection
Privacy, we are told, is the privilege of the rich. While this may be so, we all need time away from the "madding crowd." Only when we learn to listen to our own bodily needs can we hope to be attuned to the needs of others. Jesus' command is to love others as we love ourselves. If we "make space" for ourselves, there's some hope that we will find space in our lives for others!

To Think About
A man should keep for himself a little backshop ... in which he establishes his true freedom.
(M. E. de Montaigne)

Prayer
Lord, may I find ways of satisfying my hunger for solitude. Amen.

February

13

"He has done all things well." (Mark 7:37)

Background
In this note of affirmation we hear echoes of
Genesis 1:31, where we read: "God looked at everything he had made, and he found it very good."
Jesus, through his ministry, brings healing and new
life to people. In this way he renews the process of
creation; he makes good whatever humankind has
ruined by sin.

Reflection
Just as the difference between the ordinary and the
extraordinary is that little word *extra,* so the difference between doing something well and doing it
badly usually comes down to a bit of extra effort.
Once we have given of our best, we can rest, happy
in the thought that we couldn't have done more. It is
often the effort that we make which determines both
our happiness as well as our success.

To Think About
Our work is but an extension of ourselves.

Prayer
Lord, I ask not for an easy life but for the strength to
live a good one. Amen.

"Where can anyone get enough bread to satisfy them here in this deserted place?" (Mark 8:4)

Background
This is a peculiar question from the disciples, who have witnessed the previous multiplication of the loaves and fish (see Mark 6:33-34). Commentators imply that Mark intends to point to Jesus as the only person who can satisfy the deep hunger of the human heart. The question also sets the scene for Jesus to evangelize both by word and deed.

Reflection
Part of our instinct for self-preservation is the security we long for through acquiring possessions. It is often the evening of our lives before we realize that material things can never bring us the contentment we long for. Contentment lies in appreciating the fact that while we may not have everything we want, we certainly have everything we need!

To Think About
Happiness is the art of making a bouquet of those flowers within reach. (B. Goddard)

Prayer
Lord, may I have less wants and a greater appreciation of what I have. Amen.

February

15

"Blessed are you who are poor ..." (Luke 6:20)

Background
There is always the danger that we may listen to something so often that we become immune to its meaning. This may be true with the beatitudes. We don't appreciate how revolutionary they are, especially in their own time. They turn our worldly values upside down. Those who are poor are who are not self-sufficient. Spiritually speaking, they are those who realize that their need for God cannot be satisfied except by God alone.

Reflection
Poverty is not a virtue and, as Christians, we are called to alleviate it wherever we can. Archbishop Helder Camera commented: "Saints may be found in slums, but we cannot retain slums in order to make them the breeding ground of saints." Blessed poverty is the poverty that lets us realize our total dependence on God for everything we have—that without God, we are nothing.

To Think About
Few, save the poor, feel for the poor. (L. E. Landon)

Prayer
Lord, help me to be a blessing for the least of your people. Amen.

"Why does this generation seek a sign?"
(Mark 8:12)

Background
Jesus uses the term "this generation" in a pejorative way, referring to those who refuse to believe in spite of seeing many signs. Jesus knows that the Pharisees act out of ill will; they do not search for truth, and no amount of proof will convince them. The situation resembles the old adage that states: "There are none so blind as those who do not wish to see."

Reflection
With the advancement of science, there is always the danger that the only truth we will accept is the one that can be verified through scientific laws and rules. We often find that when the need for proof enters, faith is forced to exit. If we choose to follow Jesus, we must be prepared to await the proof of the things he promises.

To Think About
Faith declares what the senses do not see.
(B. Paschal)

Prayer
Lord, help me to keep my eyes fixed on you today. Amen.

February

17

"And do you not remember?" (Mark 8:18b)

Background

The concept of "remembering" is central to the
Jewish faith, especially to the covenant that God
makes with his people. In Deuteronomy the
Israelites are asked to remember the saving acts of
God in the past and to see them as the basis for
their continued fidelity to the covenant (see 4:9ff).
In the New Testament Jesus tells his disciples to
remember what he did with the loaves of bread
when he fed the multitudes, and urges them to see
this as a promise of his continued care.

Reflection

If we do not remember the past we are in danger of
repeating its mistakes. By the same token, if we
remember the blessings we have been given, we will
never doubt the goodness of God. We are told that
Jesus Christ does not change; he is the same yesterday, today, and forever (see Hebrews 13:8). If Jesus
has helped us through thick and thin in the past, will
he not see us through the difficulties that lie ahead?

To Think About

Eaten bread is soon forgotten.

Prayer

For what has been, thank you; for all that is yet to
come, thank you. Amen.

"I see people looking like trees and walking."
(Mark 8:24)

Background
Blindness has always been a curse in Eastern countries. It is caused by various eye diseases and is compounded by the constant glare of the sun. In the time of Jesus, lack of hygiene helps spread the various illnesses from one person to another. In this instance, it appears that the man's gradual growth in faith is the reason for the miracle working gradually.

Reflection
A little boy was asked in catechism class: "If we are the believers, who are the unbelievers?" The little boy answered, "Those who do not fight over religion." If we see people as "others," we will probably treat them as we would treat the stones along the road. If we see "others" as our brothers and sisters, they become a part of us and will be treated accordingly.

To Think About
He who plants kindness will reap love.

Prayer
Lord, may I see you reflected in every person I meet today, regardless of the differences that might appear to separate us. Amen.

"But who do you say that I am?" (Mark 8:29)

Background

This question comes at a strategic moment in Mark's Gospel. Opposition to Jesus' ministry is gathering force, and it is only a matter of time before there will be outright persecution. The question represents a minor identity crisis for Jesus. He is wondering what effect he is having and what, if anything, he has achieved.

Reflection

Much will depend on the answer we give to the question: "Who is Jesus for me?" Consequently, it is worth resting with. Our answer will change as our relationship with Jesus grows. During the course of our life, it will probably move from seeing Jesus as a type of teddy bear, someone we turn to in times of distress, to the point where we can honestly answer: "You are my God and my all!"

To Think About

Who is Jesus for me?

Prayer

Lord, draw me closer to you each day. Amen.

"For whoever wishes to save his life will lose it ..."
(Mark 8:35)

Background
Jesus is becoming increasingly aware of the persecution that looms larger with each passing day. He calls his followers to walk the path that he is about to tread himself: the path of suffering. He leaves none of his followers in any doubt of what will be asked of them if they decide to answer "yes" to his invitation to follow him.

Reflection
The effort that some species of butterflies have to make to break out from the cocoon is a vital part of their development. Without the struggle, their ability to survive in the world will be retarded. A vital part of our spiritual growth is the effort we make to reach out and help others. It is in living for others that we grow beyond ourselves, whereas if we concentrate on our own happiness, our growth as human beings will be retarded.

To Think About
It is in giving to others that I receive.

Prayer
Lord, may I realize that I can serve you in serving those about me. Amen.

February

21

"Rabbi, it is good that we are here!" (Mark 9:5)

Background

The transfiguration is a traumatic experience for the disciples. Jesus has just told them that he is going to Jerusalem where he will meet his fate, and this has a shattering effect on them. Within a short time they are going to be the ones who witness the passion. The experience of the transfiguration will have to sustain them for a long time.

Reflection

God has the knack of putting us where he needs us. Yet, so often we think that we should be elsewhere, doing something different—usually something we think is much more important. Realizing that we're where God wants us to be may not make our work easier; in fact, it may make it even more demanding. If we can remember that we are where God wants us to be, however, it will add an extra dimension to life.

To Think About

"The place where you stand is holy ground." (Exodus 3:5)

Prayer

Lord, may I realize that you depend on me to do your work as I depend on you. Amen.

"Love your enemies, do good to those who hate you." (Luke 6:27)

February
22

Background
The Greek word used here for "love" is *agapan*. This is the kind of love that does not take into consideration what we think of the person or what the person has done to us in the past; we will work for nothing but that person's highest good. This love has little to do with the heart and everything to do with the will. In this instance, love is a conscious decision that we make for the other person and for his or her well being.

Reflection
Love not expressed by deeds is suspect. While it may be relatively easy to speak well of our enemies, it's more difficult to translate those words into actions. Love and forgiveness expressed in acts cannot be refuted and it seldom needs an explanation. Ultimately, it is our actions that speak far more clearly than any words we may happen to utter.

To Think About
The way to destroy my enemies is to shower them with kindness.

Prayer
Lord, forgive me my trespasses, just as I forgive those who trespass against me. Amen.

February

23

"Bring him to me." (Mark 9:19)

Background
This short phrase expresses a sense of exasperation on the part of Jesus, because his disciples are not proving to be as effective as he might have wished. Jesus confronts the boy's father about his apparent lack of faith, and leads him to a faith that is the pre-requisite for healing. It is faith that enables us to tap into the power of God.

Reflection
There is a rather cynical expression which says: "When all else fails, try prayer!" For some people, there is an element of truth in this because they turn to Jesus as a last resort, rather than as a first. Yet, Jesus invites us: "Come to me, all you who labor and are burdened, and I will give you rest" (Matthew 11:28). If, as we are told, a burden shared is a burden halved, then who better to help us than Jesus?

To Think About
I hope that the cross I carry is that of Jesus.

Prayer
Jesus, I place all my trust in you. Amen.

"Whoever receives one child such as this in my name, receives me. . . ." (Mark 9:37)

Background
Aware that his disciples are discussing who among them is the greatest, Jesus begins teaching about the true meaning of greatness. The great person is the one who is prepared to be last, for that person will be first. The one who wants to be first must be servant of all. Some commentators maintain that in this particular phrase Jesus is teaching his disciples how they should treat others.

Reflection
Even with great planning, parents could never determine the precise children that God gives them. Rather, children are given as gifts—warts and all! Since God speaks in a unique way through each person he creates, children are his special message to their parents. If parents listen to their children— in what their children say and don't say—they will come to see the creation of God at work in a way they never dreamed possible.

To Think About
The time spent in forming children is our gift to posterity.

Prayer
Lord, may I see you even in the smallest part of your creation. Amen.

February 25

"But when you give alms, do not let your left hand know what your right is doing."
(Matthew 6:3)

Background

Prayer, fasting, and almsgiving are the three expressions of personal piety among the chosen people. Many choose to fast on market days, when they are assured of a large audience of admirers. Jesus confronts this situation and teaches that genuine piety does not have a hidden agenda—the praise of those about us, for example!

Reflection

Before we can open our hearts to receive blessings that God wants to give us, we have to let go of what we're clasping—and for many of us, what we clasp may be pride. It's difficult to open a heart that is already full. It may be that we are called to travel life's pathway a bit more lightly by being a bit more humble. As we give, let it be done in a spirit of humble simplicity and anonymity. Simplicity and anonymity will ensure that the one who counts does, indeed, see.

To Think About

Living more simply often enables another to simply live.

Prayer

Lord, help me to share the blessings I have received. Amen.

"If anyone wants to come after me, he must deny himself and take up his cross daily and follow me." (Luke 9:23)

Background
Jesus is in the process of teaching his followers the true meaning of what the role of the Messiah entails, which has little to do with pomp and ceremony. At the center of the Messiah's mission, in fact, lies the cross—and Jesus' listeners know only too well what this involves. Not only is the cross central to the role of the Messiah but it must cast its shadow across the lives of all his followers.

Reflection
German martyr Dietrich Bonhoeffer wrote that when Jesus calls someone to follow him, he bids that person to come and die. While Christ spends only three hours on the cross, his suffering is reflective of his entire life. Although life is not meant to be one long crucifixion, trying to live the Christian life without the cross is tantamount to trying to swim in a pool empty of water.

To Think About
What is it costing me to be a disciple of Jesus?

Prayer
Lord, grant me joy and strength to do your will. Amen.

February

26

"Can the wedding guests mourn as long as the bridegroom is with them?" (Matthew 9:15a)

Background
A wedding is not a one-day affair in Jesus' culture. Rather, the celebrations usually last a week or longer. Instead of going away for a honeymoon, the bride and groom spend time with their guests, who are treated to a time of merriment. Nothing but joyfulness and rejoicing are part of the celebration.

Reflection
Even though there may be sickness or hardship, there is a sense of inner peace when Jesus is present. Father Faber, the poet, wrote: "Ill that he blesses is our good and unblessed good is ill. / All is right that seems most wrong if it be his sweet will." These words highlight Saint Paul's assurance: "If God is for us, who can be against us?" (Romans 8:31)

To Think About
I invite Jesus to feast and celebrate within my own soul.

Prayer
Lord, remind me that there is nothing that can happen today that we cannot handle together. Amen.

"I have not come to call the righteous to repentance but sinners." (Luke 5:32)

February

28

Background
Jesus calls Matthew, the tax collector, to become his follower. At the time of Jesus, tax collectors are regarded as human pariahs and outcasts and, as such, are not allowed into the synagogue. They have a similar social status to that of robbers and murderers. It is to these, the rejected ones, that Jesus wishes to offer a new way of life.

Reflection
Even though we may fail to recognize it, what we experience as the cross is often our greatest gift. However, like many gifts, it may be so well wrapped that we fail to recognize it as gift. If we didn't have a struggle in our lives, would we have any need for a savior? Quite often the struggle, or the cross, can be the stepping stone that brings us closer to Jesus. Because it is too much for us to handle alone, we turn to him.

To Think About
"Come to me, all you who labor and are burdened, and I will give you rest." (Matthew 11:28)

Prayer
Lord, I know you are within me and there is nothing I shall fear. Amen.

February

29

"Depart from me, Lord, for I am a sinful man."
(Luke 5:8)

Background
Peter's response to Jesus is both a confession, in which he acknowledges Jesus' lordship, and a declaration, in which he realizes his personal unworthiness to be in the company of Jesus. The change from the use of "Master" to "Lord" shows the religious fear that Peter experiences before the awesome presence of the divine.

Reflection
A race driver pointed out that two rules are essential in the sport of racing. The first is to know your car; the second is to know your limitations. Peter grows in the appreciation of what he is called to be, and he knows just how frail he is. Because of this, he learns to trust in Jesus and to become the rock on whom Jesus founds his church. It is often in our weakness that God's strength is most evident.

To Think About
Where love is thick, faults appear thin.

Prayer
Lord, may my heart be humble in the presence of your divine love.

"One does not live by bread alone."
(Luke 4:4)

Background
This particular phrase is taken from Deuteronomy 8:3, which was considered by many to be the favorite book of the Old Testament for the early Christian Church. It tells us that a person will never find satisfaction in material things. Jesus knows this, of course, yet the wilderness in which his temptation takes place is full of stones that look like loaves of bread—and he is hungry.

Reflection
Most of the "greats" who have fallen have done so because of an abuse of pleasure, power, or possessions—the three great stumbling blocks to living a Christ-like life. When used correctly, pleasure, power, and possessions can give a special quality to life. When they are abused, however, disastrous consequences follow; instead of being their masters we become their slaves.

To Think About
Character can be judged by what persons do when they are not being watched.

Prayer
Lord, melt me, mold me, and fashion me. Amen.

"Whatever you did for one of these least brothers of mine, you did for me." (Matthew 25:40b)

Background

We can summarize the whole of this passage by saying that people are judged solely on their behavior toward their fellow human beings. The behavior mentioned is nothing extraordinary; rather, it is the simple task of caring for others: feeding the hungry, giving a drink to the thirsty, making a stranger welcome, visiting the sick or imprisoned—all of which are services anyone can render—all of which are services to Jesus!

Reflection

When Jesus came among us on the first Christmas, he came disguised—and he still does! We can be sure that whenever we meet brothers or sisters in need, we are meeting Jesus. And to totally confuse us, these brothers and sisters usually come at the most inconvenient times. However, that moment of inconvenience is the one time we are most certain of meeting Jesus.

To Think About

Can I afford to let Jesus touch me through a brother or sister in need? Can I afford not to?

Prayer

Lord, give me a heart that can see—a heart that will love. Amen.

"If you forgive others their transgressions, your heavenly Father will forgive you." (Matthew 6:14)

Background
Jesus is teaching his followers that the only limitation we can place on God's forgiveness of us is our forgiveness of others. It is the law of diminishing returns, whereby if we sow sparingly we will reap sparingly.

Reflection
Ideally, we are called to understand the reason for a person's behavior and, with this understanding, to forgive the injury we've suffered. We must never forget, however, that forgiveness is a decision. We forgive someone through an act of the will. Many have said that Jesus' teaching on forgiveness is the most difficult part of Christianity because it is in direct contrast to what our world teaches. Yet, forgiveness lies at the heart of Christian teaching.

To Think About
Robert Bridges, the English poet laureate, said: "To forgive was the sign of a great person, but to forget was sublime." While I may never achieve the sublime, I can decide to be great. The choice is mine.

Prayer
Lord, when I bury the hatchet with another, help me to not mark the spot. Amen.

March

4

"This generation is an evil generation; it seeks a sign, but no sign will be given it, except the sign of Jonah." (Luke 11:29b)

Background

Jonah journeys from Palestine to the Assyrian town of Nineveh to preach repentance. Even though the Ninevites are pagans, they listen to what Jonah has to say and are converted to God. In Jesus, there is someone far greater than Jonah, and yet the Jews refuse to believe in him and to bring about the repentance he preaches. They want entertainment not repentance!

Reflection

When Shakespeare wrote, "The world is too much with us, getting and spending we lay waste our power," he spoke a truth that is far more relevant now than it was in his time. Because of the rat race we are a part of, we are in danger of losing the poetic streak that lies within all of us. It will be interesting to see, in years to come, how many mystics our age produces.

To Think About

There is still time to learn to smell the roses and to listen to the tree tell its story.

Prayer

Lord, open my eyes to see you in the bits and pieces of today. Amen.

"Ask and it will be given to you; seek and you will find; knock and the door will be opened to you."
(Matthew 7:7)

Background
In Greek there are two mandatory forms of the verb. One is called the aorist imperative, which is usually used when a definite command is being given, such as "Speak up." The second is the present imperative, which usually connotes a continuous command, such as "One should always speak up." It is the second form of the verb that is used in this text, implying that one should continue "asking," "seeking," and "knocking."

Reflection
Any parent knows that it is not always good to give children what they ask for, because children don't realize that what they want may prove to be harmful to them. In much the same way, people often feel that their prayers go unanswered because they don't receive what they ask for. If God is our Father, maybe we would be better served in trusting him for what we need!

To Think About
If God were to answer my prayer, could I live with the results?

Prayer
Father, open the right doors and close the wrong ones. Amen.

March

6

"Leave your gift there at the altar, go first and be reconciled." (Matthew 5:24)

Background
Sacrifice within the Jewish thinking is a means of restoring a proper relationship between human beings and God. However, if a sin is deliberately committed, the sacrifice is powerless until the person tries to make retribution for the effects of the sin.

Reflection
Jesus always identifies himself with the neighbor. "Whatever you did for one of these least brothers of mine, you did for me" (Matthew 25:40). The greatest obstacle to our offering worship to God is our failure to be at one with those about us. Before we can make the upward journey to God, we must first make an outward one to the brothers and sisters about us, beginning with forgiveness.

To Think About
When we are not afraid to confess our own poverty, we will be able to be with other people in theirs. (Henri Nouwen)

Prayer
Lord, that I may be willing to journey toward my neighbor with forgiveness. Amen.

"Love your enemies." (Matthew 5:44)

Background
The Greek word for "love" used in this passage is *agape,* which can be translated as "desiring what's best for the loved one." This kind of love has little to do with feelings or emotions, and is very much concerned with an act of the will, whereby we try to overcome the hostile feelings we have for those who have wronged us.

Reflection
To love someone involves more than mere superficial thinking and feeling. Rather, love is proved by deeds. Consequently, if we are to love our enemies, we will put ourselves at their service. This is what makes "love your enemies" the most difficult command contained in Christianity. Who are the people we, as Christians, are pledged to serve?

To Think About
In the evening of our life we will be judged by love. (Saint John of the Cross)

Prayer
Lord, teach me to love. Amen.

March

8

While he was praying his face changed in appearance.... (Luke 9:29)

Background

Jesus has just "set his face towards Jerusalem," which means that he is going to confront the Jewish religious authorities. He knows the danger in this. While we will never know what actually happened during the transfiguration, we do see Jesus going aside to consult the Father before he faces the trials ahead of him. Jesus never does anything without first consulting the Father.

Reflection

In the play *Macbeth,* Shakespeare wrote, "There's no art to find the mind's construction in the face," which means we cannot determine what people are thinking merely by looking at them. However, when we become people of prayer, we become God-centered people who want only what God wants and who recognize his hand in everything we see. This brings us a security and contentment no money can buy.

To Think About

Prayer is more a matter of us listening to God rather than God listening to us.

Prayer

Lord, may my prayer lead me to see you in the beauty of nature and humankind. Amen.

"Be merciful, just as [also] your Father is merciful." (Luke 6:36)

Background
In the Old Testament, mercy is reserved for God alone. In this passage, Jesus is exhorting his followers to love their enemies (see Luke 6:27), which sheds light on what it means to be merciful. It implies that no matter what others do to us or how they treat us, we desire nothing for them but what will accrue to their good.

Reflection
By nature we are inclined to dominate others. This often shows up in our efforts to exact vengeance on others when they fall short of our expectations of them. To be merciful toward others necessitates reversing the roles. Before we can dare pass sentence on another, we must first examine ourselves. Such honest self-examination can not only change our perspective, but we experience a change of heart. Jesus does just that for us. He takes our condemnation on himself and dies for us.

To Think About
I pray for those I like the least, for they are the ones who need God the most.

Prayer
Lord, change my heart so that I can change my view of others. Amen.

"They tie up heavy burdens [hard to carry] and lay them on people's shoulders, but they will not lift a finger to move them." (Matthew 23:4)

Background
The influence of Pharisaic theory and practice on the way the Law is interpreted leads to severe practices. At times, even some of the rabbis themselves are critical of the austerity with which the Law is interpreted. We find such criticism not only in the Gospels but also in such contemporary writings as the Talmud.

Reflection
A young naval officer, given the responsibility of taking a destroyer out of port, so organized things that the task was accomplished in record time. As he silently commended himself for how well he fulfilled his task, the officer was handed a radio message from the captain: "Congratulations on your feat! Next time, try to make sure that the captain is on board when you leave!" It is possible to do things perfectly while forgetting those for whom we are doing them.

To Think About
My greatest achievements are those that are accomplished for the benefit others.

Prayer
Lord, may everything I do be done with compassion. Amen.

"Whoever wishes to be great among you shall be your servant." (Matthew 20:26)

Background

Jesus is teaching his followers about the true meaning of power and authority. Absolute power is not to be used by those who are in positions of leadership within the Church. Rather, within the Church, social positions are reversed; leaders are those who must fill the role of servant, while those who are least are to be seen as those who are truly important.

Reflection

In the unlikely event that Christians were to decide to replace the cross as the Christian symbol, they would find nothing more meaningful and significant than the towel and washing bowl. When Jesus attempts to teach his disciples the kernel of what is involved in following him, he washes their feet and commands that they should do this for one another (see John 13:14). This is his way of showing that service is at the core of discipleship and that love is at the heart of service.

To Think About

The heart is at its best when it's pumping for others.

Prayer

May I count it a privilege to serve you in others. Amen.

March

12

"Remember that you received what was good during your lifetime." (Luke 16:25)

Background

The story of Dives and Lazarus transcends both time and culture. The name Dives comes from the Latin word meaning "rich," while Lazarus is a Latin version of Eleazar, which means "God is my help." Dives eventually experiences torment not because he is rich but because he is unwilling to reach out and help; he simply does nothing!

Reflection

The Argentine golfer, Robert de Vincenzo, had just won a major tournament and was approached by a lady who asked him to help her and her baby, who was sick with a rare disease. De Vincenzo endorsed his winnings check and gave it to the woman. He learned later that the woman was a fraud; there was no sick baby. De Vincenzo replied: "No sick baby! That's the best news that I've heard all week."

To Think About

Riches are neither good nor bad; it's what I do with them that matters.

Prayer

May I realize, Lord, that there are no pockets in a burial shroud. Amen.

"The kingdom of God will be taken away from you and given to a people that will produce its fruit." (Matthew 21:43)

Background
The parable of the vineyard is significant for the Jews who think of themselves as the "vineyard of the Lord of hosts" (see Isaiah 5:7). While God is shown to be a God of infinite patience, there does come a time of judgment. The most tragic judgment God can make is when he removes from us the very task he entrusted to us and gives it to another.

Reflection
The foreman of a building firm had cheated on his company for most of his life by using inferior materials and charging top prices. When the time for his retirement came, his boss asked him to build one last house. Knowing that this was to be his final opportunity to make some easy money, he cut every conceivable corner. At his farewell party, the company presented the man with the keys to the house he had just built!

To Think About
Happiness has more to do with my disposition than with my position in life.

Prayer
Lord, when I'm wrong, may I demand change in myself; when I'm right, may I be slow in demanding it in others. Amen.

March

14

"Father, I have sinned against heaven and against you." (Luke 15:18b)

Background
The preceding parables of the lost sheep and the lost coin set the scene for this parable. This parable, however, is a type of climax, since what is lost and found is a human being. Jesus' listeners have no problem seeing the role of the sinner (the younger brother), the Pharisee (the older brother), and God (the prodigal father).

Reflection
Acknowledging our sin means realizing its implications. Sin is always a triangle. It involves God, our neighbor, and ourselves. To omit any one of these is to underestimate the enormous dimension of sin. So often we downplay sin with the justification: "I'm not hurting anyone but myself." Just as a chain is as strong as its weakest link, so the health of the Christian family depends on our doing our own individual part to ensure that we do not damage the health of the body of Christ through sin.

To Think About
When another feels that there's a possibility of forgiveness, they may be moved to seek it.

Prayer
Lord, may I realize that when I forgive another, I actually set myself free. Amen.

"... it may bear fruit in the future." (Luke 13:9a)

Background

The tree in question is Israel, the chosen people. Even though it fails to bear fruit by responding to the message that Jesus comes to bring, Jesus does not believe that the Jews ultimately will reject him. God waits patiently for fruit to appear, whether this is within the life of the individual or within the chosen people as a whole.

Reflection

It is said that hope springs eternal. Nowhere is this seen more clearly than in the lives of people. How often we witness the most hardened criminals changing their ways. Unfortunately, we tend to give up on people and "write them off," instead of entrusting them to God. It takes a lifetime for God to complete his act of creation, and we know that he doesn't create rubbish!

To Think About

I must be patient with my neighbors; God hasn't finished with them yet.

Prayer

Lord, remind me about who is in charge of this day. Amen.

March

16

"No prophet is accepted in his own native place."
(Luke 4:24)

Background

This phrase is part of the passage that focuses on Jesus' rejection of a purely Jewish mission and the unfavorable reaction this receives. Jesus pays a compliment to the Gentiles, much to the disgust of the Jews, who pride themselves in being God's chosen people to the exclusion of all others.

Reflection

When we get to know others we tend to put them in neat compartments that allow us to feel secure. Often we resent it, then, when they break out of the straitjackets we've placed about them. To be human is to grow and to grow is to change. To be able to accept change in others is to acknowledge that God is still in the process of creating.

To Think About

If I were put on trial for being Christian, would there be enough evidence to prove me guilty?

Prayer

Lord, may I learn to recognize and rejoice in the miracles you work in my life. Amen.

"Moved with compassion . . ." (Matthew 18:27a)

Background
In contrasting the king, who is willing to cancel the
large debt that the servant owes him, with the servant, who is unwilling to make the slightest
allowance to the one who owes him an insignificant
sum of money, Jesus is emphasizing the extent of
God's forgiveness. This, in turn, has to be the model
for us. The quality that makes such forgiveness
possible is compassion.

Reflection
The first step in coming to forgive others is to understand them. Once we understand the circumstances
of their lives, we will find it easier to love them and
eventually forgive them. Compassion, the ability to
suffer with another, enables us to take that first step.
Compassion trains the eye to see the loveliness of
God in unexpected events, places, and people.

To Think About
For better or for worse, I am my brother's and my
sister's keeper!

Prayer
Lord, may yours be the image that is reflected in
each face I see this day. Amen.

March

18

"Whoever obeys and teaches these commandments will be called greatest in the kingdom of heaven." *(Matthew 5:19)*

Background

Realizing the powerlessness of the Law, when taken as an end in itself, Jesus tells his disciples that it is submission to the will of God that is important. This is something that goes beyond the mere external observance of the Law. The observance of the Law is intended to lead one to fulfill the wishes of God. As Saint Teresa of Avila said: "Ideally, the Law should point us toward the heart of God."

Reflection

We are told that our Church needs witnesses to the gospel in a way that it has never needed them before. It is a difficult vocation and, in spite of our best efforts, we often appear to get nowhere. Most of our lives are ordinary and humdrum and appear to achieve very little. However, we must never forget, as Saint Thérèse of Lisieux says, "We're not called to be successful; we are called to be faithful!" It's the daily living of the gospel message that will eventually determine our greatness.

To Think About

The greatest aspect of my life is its ordinariness.

Prayer

Lord, keep me on the right path today. Amen.

". . . he will save his people from their sins."
(Matthew 1:21)

March

19

Background
Jesus is the Greek form of the Jewish name "Joshua,"
and *Joshua*, the Hebrew root of Jesus' name, means
"God is savior." From the outset, through the name
that was given to him, the purpose of Jesus' mission
is made clear. He comes as Savior, as the one who
saves us from the consequences of our sins.

Reflection
Someone remarked that a sin only feels like a sin the
first time that we commit it! The danger with sin is
that it can easily become a habit. Scripture, however,
offers a way of life that is free of sin and that will
bring its own rewards. Saint Joseph is an example of
one who lives this way of life. He doesn't have an
easy life but he quietly does much to further the
work of God and thereby live a fulfilled life.

To Think About
"If you knew the gift of God . . . you would have
asked him and he would have given you living
water." (John 4:10)

Prayer
Lord, may my heart remain restless until it rests in
you. Amen.

March

20

"You shall love your neighbor as yourself."
(Mark 12:31)

Background
Jesus says that he has come not to destroy the Law but to fulfil it. We see an example of that here. This quotation, based on Leviticus 19:18, pertains only to fellow Jews. Jews are entitled to hate Gentiles if they so wish. Jesus does not place such a restriction on who our neighbor is, however; he enlarges the meaning of the word "neighbor" to include all humankind.

Reflection
Many of us fail to love our neighbor because we fail to love ourselves. It seems that when we're feeling good about ourselves, our neighbor doesn't present too much of a problem. By the same token, when we're out of sorts with ourselves, our neighbor receives rough justice from us. Since we cannot give what we do not have, we must learn to accept and love ourselves before we can hope to accept and love another.

To Think About
God created me and God doesn't make junk!

Prayer
Thank you, Lord, for loving me just as I am. Amen.

"O God, be merciful to me a sinner" (Luke 18:13b)

March

21

Background

This passage comes at the end of Jesus' teaching about prayer. Jesus tells the parable of the Pharisee and the tax collector to teach one of the central principles on which genuine prayer is founded: We stand before God as sinners. Elsewhere we're told: "Every proud man is an abomination to the Lord" (Proverbs 16:5). Consequently, this person's prayer will never be heard.

Reflection

John of Saint Sampson wrote: "To know oneself is the greatest knowledge of all. It is more valuable to know the beauty of one's own self than to know how excellent are the angels, how wide the heavens. Real self is an awareness of being a reality different from the pressures of outsiders and of being more than the inner pressures of instincts and emotions."

To Think About

Sin has been defined as loving someone or something more than God. Where is the love of my life?

Prayer

Lord, be merciful to me and hear my prayer, for I am a sinner. Amen.

March

22

"So he got up and went back to his father."
(Luke 15:20a)

Background

When the prodigal son returns to his father, he pleads to be taken back not as a son but as a hired servant who is the lowest form of slave. While the ordinary slave is practically a member of the family, the hired servant is only employed for the day and, therefore, has no standing whatsoever in the household. That person is the lowest of the low.

Reflection

An elderly farmer was enjoying an afternoon nap in his rocking chair on the veranda of his house when a young sales executive jumped out of his car with a book in his hand. Rushing up to the farmer the salesman said, "Sir, this book will teach you what you need to do in order to get a greater return from your land." Opening one eye, the farmer replied: "Young man, I already know what I need to do to get a greater yield from my land—work harder!"

To Think About

The way to hell is paved with good intentions—and when I act on my good intentions, it becomes my way to heaven!

Prayer

Lord, enable me to act today so that I can change tomorrow. Amen.

The man believed what Jesus said to him.
(John 4:50b)

Background

The miracle at Cana is recorded just before this passage, which deals with the healing of the royal official's son in Capernaum. In both instances, Jesus' initial response appears to be a refusal. Jesus wants to move his followers away from a faith that is founded solely on miracles. The official recognizes that the refusal is not final, however, and we find him believing what Jesus says. The eventual cure becomes the fruit of the man's faith, not the cause of it.

Reflection

It is said that most Christians believe the Good News is too good to be true. How many times do we limit the power of Jesus to work his miracles because we fail to take him at his word; we fail to believe that he can enable us to achieve the impossible. This happens even in Jesus' own hometown (see Matthew 3:58). For those who wish to be Christian, Jesus must be an active participant and companion within their lives, not a mere hero.

To Think About

Some say that Christianity has failed; perhaps it has yet to be tried!

Prayer

Lord, I believe. Help thou my unbelief. Amen.

"Do you want to be well?" *(John 5:6b)*

Background
It is most likely that Jesus visits the pool of Bethesda
while he is in Jerusalem for one of the major Jewish
feasts. Bethesda is a district that covers almost one
quarter of Jerusalem. At the time, people believe that
spirits and demons exist in certain places, such as in
the wilderness, in trees, and in streams. Beneath the
pool of Bethesda there is probably a stream that
occasionally bubbles and disturbs the waters. It is
no problem for the people to believe that this is the
work of a spirit.

Reflection
Before we ask for anything in prayer, it might be good
for us to think about what it is we're asking for and
the possible consequences should we receive it. Once
his prayer is answered, the paralytic finds that his life
is radically changed. He suddenly finds himself out of
a job, for he can no longer beg for alms as a cripple.
From now on he will have to work for a living!

To Think About
Would I be able to live with the consequences of my
prayers if they were answered?

Prayer
Lord, I trust that you know what is best for me.
Amen.

"Hail, favored one! The Lord is with you."
(Luke 1:28)

Background

Taken literally, the Greek text translates "hail" as "rejoice!" Although the term "The Lord is with you" can be taken as a simple greeting, it is significant here, as Mary is given a unique mission. She is the instrument, chosen by God, through whom his love for the world will become incarnated in the person of Jesus Christ.

Reflection

We cannot hope to communicate love to others unless we have first experienced love ourselves. God's love is mediated to us through those significant people he places in our lives—people who love us with all our faults. To the extent that we are open to being loved by others, we are open to God's love—and when we experience God's unconditional love, we are in a better position to share love with others.

To Think About

Experiencing God's love is the difference between living and existing.

Prayer

Open my heart, Lord, to the depth of your love for me. Amen.

"You do not want to come to me to have life."
(John 5:40)

Background

This verse comes at the end of a passage in which
Jesus, having extolled the testimony of John the
Baptist, speaks of himself as being an even greater
witness. He is a greater witness because the Father
testifies on his behalf. Jesus then moves to the
Jewish leaders' disbelief, which he claims is willful.

Reflection

When will we believe that Jesus came that we might
have life and have it to the full (see John 10:10)? The
invitation is given to us each day but nobody can
respond on our behalf. As the psalmist says: "That
today, if you would hear his voice: Do not harden
your hearts" (see Psalm 95:7-8).

To Think About

No Jesus, know fear. Know Jesus, no fear!

Prayer

Lord, you have the message of eternal life. Amen.

"He is speaking openly and they say nothing to him." (John 7:26a)

March

27

Background
Because of his preaching, Jesus incurs the wrath of the authorities. Here we find him preaching openly in the Temple. Solomon's Porch and the Royal Porch are two sections of the Temple where rabbis teach and people are free to move from one teacher to another. This episode probably occurs here. In spite of Jesus' claims, the people are taken aback by the fact that the authorities don't question or confront him.

Reflection
Prejudice (pre-judging) is said to be the chain that binds us and blinds us without our knowing. Prejudices are a part of our conditioning over the years. Time and again we find that we dismiss people and their ideas without first taking the time to listen to them and understand what they are trying to communicate. The most unfortunate aspect of our prejudices is that frequently we are unaware of them or even deny their existence. Often it's a question of everybody else being out of step—except me!

To Think About
What difference would it make if Jesus were removed from my life tomorrow?

Prayer
Lord, that I might see myself as others see me. Amen.

"*Does our law condemn a person before it first hears him and finds out what he is doing?*"
(John 7:51)

Background

The net of the religious authorities is tightening around Jesus. Nicodemus, who secretly comes to Jesus by night, takes a rather timid stance before the rest of the Sanhedrin. He refers to the Law (see Exodus 23:1; Deuteronomy 1:6) which states that every man must receive justice. This justice necessitates that persons be given the opportunity of presenting and defending their position; no person can be condemned on rumors or hearsay.

Reflection

To understand persons' actions we must first "stand under" them by attempting to put ourselves in their place to see things from their perspective. An old proverb says that we must first walk a mile in another's moccasins before we can stand in judgment of that person. Jesus assures us that if we judge not, then we will not be judged (see Luke 6:37).

To Think About

It is often better to light a candle than to curse the dark.

Prayer

Lord, it's for me to understand and for you to judge. Amen.

"Let the one among you who is without sin be the first to throw a stone at her." *(John 8:7b)*

March

29

Background
In reply to those who bring the woman who is caught in the act of committing adultery, Jesus refers to the way in which stoning is carried out. In Deuteronomy 17:7, we read of how those who have actually witnessed the wrongdoing have to throw the first stones and then others join in.

Reflection
There's an old saying that if all of our sins were to be written on our faces, we would prefer to meet with a blind man than a scholar. So often we find it easier to gloat over the downfall of a colleague than to rejoice with that person when he or she achieves something worthwhile. It seems to be a part of our human, sinful condition. It is only when we learn to love that we learn to treat the brother or sister as ourselves—in both their misfortunes and fortunes.

To Think About
To err is human, to forgive is divine. (A. Pope)

Prayer
Father, forgive me my narrow-heartedness. Amen.

March

30

"You judge by appearances . . ." (John 8:15a)

Background

The judgment made by the scribes and Pharisees is not the same as that of Jesus, because they judge only on what they see at a human level. So often, however, the most important facts of a person's life lie deep within and can easily be missed. Jesus sees inside a person and knows a person's true intentions and worth.

Reflection

We're told that to be beautiful at the age of twenty-one is an accomplishment of the body, whereas to be beautiful at the age of sixty is an accomplishment of the soul. We need more than our eyes to recognize beauty; we need our ears, our minds, and especially our hearts, for only with the heart can we see what's truly beautiful.

To Think About

The eyes of the soul should not be hindered by the eyes of the body. (R. Benson)

Prayer

Lord, that I may see. Amen.

"I always do what is pleasing to him." (John 8:29b)

March

31

Background

This forms part of Jesus' attempt to explain to the Jews just who he is and what his mission entails. In a nutshell, Jesus is stating that the Father has always been present with him, something that has continually shown itself in the way Jesus goes about doing the work of his Father. It is the perfect underpinning of his life of total obedience.

Reflection

Sometimes we think of the Christian way of life as being somewhat of a killjoy. Saint Teresa of Avila said that before her conversion she thought that the way to hell was heaven, i.e., wine, men, and song. By the same token she thought that the way to heaven was hell, i.e., where one had to be on one's best behavior all the time. After her conversion she realized that the way to hell was, in fact, hell on earth and, by the same token, the way to heaven was heaven on earth.

To Think About

A diamond is no more than a chunk of coal that stuck to its job.

Prayer

Lord, may my lifestyle reflect the prayer of my heart. Amen.

April

1

"Everyone who commits sin is a slave of sin."
(John 8:34)

Background

Because the Jews are governed by oppressive Roman rule and their ancestors had been captives in Babylon, freedom is vitally important to them. The idea of any Jew being a slave is anathema and, consequently, for Jesus to mention being a slave and being a Jew in the same breath is highly insulting. Jesus, however, is merely stating that the one who does not sin is the only person who is truly free.

Reflection

To sin is to deliberately choose something other than what Jesus wants for us. We usually sin because it is our misguided way of seeking happiness. From experience, we know that sin, in fact, does not bring happiness; neither does it give true freedom. If we fail to develop the discipline necessary for doing the right thing, we soon become slaves to our passions.

To Think About

Sin begins like a cobweb and becomes like a steel rope.

Prayer

Lord, may my actions enable me to become the person you created me to be. Amen.

"If I glorify myself, my glory is worth nothing."
(John 8:54a)

April

2

Background
In the passage leading up to this statement, Jesus claims that he has come to bring life in all of its fullness. Here he is making the simple but profound statement that while the world may honor the successful person, all true honor must come from God and, often, that honor will not be seen this side of the grave.

Reflection
It has been said that nothing improves our sense of hearing like praise! Within all of us there is the need to be recognized; it is part of our need to be accepted and loved. However, the call of the gospel is that we should not allow our right hand to know what our left hand is doing when it comes to working for the Lord. In fact, Jesus tells us that if we trumpet our own good works, we will lose any reward we might otherwise have gained in heaven (see Matthew 6:4).

To Think About
The deed is all, the glory nothing.
(J. Wolfgang von Goethe)

Prayer
Lord, may I labor for you without asking for any reward. Amen.

"Scripture cannot be set aside." (John 10:35b)

Background

In an effort to establish who he is and the mission he has come to accomplish, Jesus debates with the Jewish rabbis. In support of his argument, Jesus uses the rabbis' method of referring to the Scriptures. On their own principles, the Jews cannot ignore the scriptural argument that is being proposed to them.

Reflection

A good book will always speak its truth, whether or not we are prepared to accept that truth. Scripture, like a good book, always confronts us with the truth. Like a mirror, Scripture reflects the quality, or the lack thereof, that is in our lives. No matter how we may try to excuse ourselves, Scripture will continue to confront us with its message. Like Christ, Scripture comforts those who are afflicted and afflicts those who are comfortable.

To Think About

Great is truth and it prevails. (Esdras 4:41)

Prayer

Be it done unto me according to thy word. Amen.

"... and there he remained with his disciples."
(John 11:54)

April

4

Background
It is quite common for Jesus to take his disciples aside for a time of reflection and teaching. In this way, he can give his disciples his undivided attention and explain the finer details of his teachings. There is another reason Jesus keeps a low profile: By his works and teachings, he is drawing the wrath of the Jewish authorities onto himself, and he needs time to let things cool down.

Reflection
Many people live with one hand reaching back to shut out regret over the past and the other hand stretching out to ward off fear of the future. In the meanwhile, they stand crucified in the present. The parting promise of Jesus is that he will not abandon us; he will be with us. If we accept this we must not fear tomorrow because he is already there.

To Think About
"I am with you always, until the end of the age."
(Matthew. 28:20)

Prayer
Lord, may I know how close you are to me. Amen.

"*Father, if you are willing, take this cup away from me.*" (Luke 22:42)

Background
The concept behind the word "cup" changes between the Old Testament and the New Testament. In the Old Testament, the word "cup" refers to the anger that God has toward those who prevent his plan for his people from working itself out. In the New Testament, the word "cup" refers to a difficult job that has to be done. Both meanings can be found in Jesus' prayer.

Reflection
It is through bearing trials that we are strengthened. As happens with Jesus, God our Father doesn't remove us from the painful situations of life; rather, he gives us the strength to endure and even to grow through them.

To Think About
God often answers "no" to our wants so that he can answer "yes" to our needs.

Prayer
Father, I look to you for the courage and strength to accept the cup that is your will. Amen.

"You always have the poor with you, but you do not always have me." (John 12:8)

April

6

Background

This is a paraphrase of Deuteronomy 15:11, "The needy will never be lacking in the land." In reply to Judas' admonition that the ointment should have been sold and the money given to the poor, Jesus says that they could help the poor at any time but that their days with him are already numbered. Jesus is exposing the hypocrisy of people who, like Judas, deceitfully profess noble motives in order to avoid giving God his due.

Reflection

It may be difficult to know when we are encountering Jesus in the bits and pieces of our daily lives. We will often find that this Jesus comes at the most inconvenient times, disguised in the smelliest of clothing and quite often making the most outlandish requests. However, he did assure us: "Whatever you did for one of these least brothers of mine, you did for me" (Matthew 25:40).

To Think About

I will not be asked what the poor did with what I gave them; rather, I will be asked if I gave!

Prayer

At the end of my day may I count my blessings. Amen.

April

7

"I will lay down my life for you." (John 13:37b)

Background
This profession of Peter's is clothed in the language of the good shepherd (see John 10:11). It is rather ironic that within a short time, it is Jesus who lays down his life for Peter. Jesus knows Peter in all of his weakness; he knows the extent to which Peter will go to save his own skin. Jesus also knows the love that Peter is capable of and the person Peter is capable of becoming.

Reflection
If the opportunity arose, many of us would seriously consider dying for Christ. A far greater problem is living for him. As the old adage says: "I love life; it's people I can't stand!" Committing our lives to Christ necessitates a daily death to our own desires. This is known as white martyrdom—as distinct from red martyrdom, which involves the shedding of one's blood. Today, if we live for him as completely as possible, we will find that many small deaths will take place.

To Think About
Today, Jesus has no other heart to love with but mine; no other hands to work with but mine.

Prayer
Lord, may I appreciate that it is in dying to myself that I am born to eternal life. Amen.

Then Judas, his betrayer, said in reply: "Surely it is not I, Rabbi?" (Matthew 26:25)

April

8

Background
Matthew is attempting to show Jesus' distinct disclosure to Judas that he knows who the traitor is. The other apostles, however, do not notice this intimation. We are not told that this knowledge causes a public condemnation of Judas. The sin that Judas is about to commit is less than Peter's; the big difference is that Peter knows that he will be forgiven, whereas Judas feels that he is beyond hope.

Reflection
One of the greatest problems we encounter in driving a vehicle is the "blind spot." Similarly, the blind spots within our character present some of our greatest difficulties on our journey of life. It is said that we see most clearly in others the faults that are greatest within ourselves. How often do we need to remind ourselves of the fact that, as J. Bradford said, "There but for the grace of God go I."

To Think About
More torturous than all else is the human heart. (Jeremiah 17:9)

Prayer
Lord, guard me as the apple of your eye. Amen.

April 9

"If I, therefore, the master and teacher, have washed your feet, you ought to wash one another's feet." (John 13:14)

Background

At the time of Jesus, the roads of Palestine are little more than dirt tracks. Depending on the time of year, these dirt roadways can be covered in inches of dust or they can be veritable mud baths. Consequently, it is customary to have large water pots at the door of one's home where a servant will be present to wash the feet of guests as they arrive. Because his disciples have argued earlier about "which of them should be regarded as the greatest" (Luke 22:24), Jesus decides to teach by example.

Reflection

Service has been described as a desire to give of oneself to another without counting the cost. True service is a rare commodity nowadays. Because it is so rare, it is all the more precious when we encounter it. The one who truly serves will usually count it a privilege to be of service to another, and the service is usually performed with grace, charm and, above all, love.

To Think About

Love is the difference between performing a duty and providing a service.

Prayer

Lord, may you minister to others through me. Amen.

He said: "It is finished." And bowing his head, he handed over the spirit. (John 19:30)

Background
When we read the Gospel of John, we must be aware that there are various layers of meaning in any given passage. While the other Evangelists speak of Jesus "expiring," John speaks of Jesus "handing over" his spirit. Some scholars see this as John's intention to have the reader think of the Spirit that is to be given as a result of Jesus' glorification.

Reflection
Someone once said that when Jesus was asked to show how much he loved them, he stretched out his arms and died. Jesus' giving is total. If we're honest, most of us have to admit that we give only from our abundance. Seldom do we really miss what we give to another, whether it is of our time or of our gifts. There is, indeed, a direct correlation between happiness and giving: It is in giving that we receive.

To Think About
How often do I give to the point that it hurts?

Prayer
Lord, remember me when you come into your kingdom. Amen.

April

11

"Who will roll back the stone for us from the entrance to the tomb?" *(Mark 16:3)*

Background

Tombs in Palestine at the time of Jesus have no doors. Rather, a large, flat, circular stone normally stands at the opening of a burial crypt. The stone is placed in a groove that allows the stone to be moved with relatively little effort. Moving the stone that is in front of Jesus' tomb, however, would be impossible for the women.

Reflection

Fear of failure so often prevents us from doing great things for God. Paul, however, wasn't shy in claiming that he could do all things because of Jesus who strengthened him (see Philippians 4:13). We have the same Jesus as our helper. The only things that prevent him from performing miracles for us is our lack of faith; we fail to give him the opportunity.

To Think About

Have no fear of what the future holds, for God holds the future.

Prayer

Lord, I fear not since you are near. Amen.

He saw and believed. (John 20:8b)

Background
When the two disciples enter the tomb, they find only the cloths in which the dead body of Jesus had been wrapped. According to the Greek text, these clothes are not thrown carelessly aside; rather, they are in their original shape, implying that the body had mysteriously moved from within them. With the body missing and the clothes positioned in the shape of the body, John interprets the scene and comes to believe that Jesus is risen.

Reflection
When we love someone, it is as if that person can do no wrong. By the same token, there are those people who, in spite of what they do, we find it difficult to see any good in them. So often it is a case of self-fulfilling prophecies. People perform as we prophesy; if we let others know that we expect great things of them, they often meet our expectations. The opposite is also true.

To Think About
For what a man would like to be true, that he more readily believes. (F. Bacon)

Prayer
Lord, may I learn to see with your eyes and to hear with your heart. Amen.

April

13

"Do not be afraid." (Matthew 28:10)

Background

While Matthew appears to have drawn on Mark's account for this apparition of Jesus, there are many differences between the two. All of the Evangelists, however, punctuate their resurrection appearances with such reassurances as "It is I" (Luke 24:39), "Peace be with you" (Luke 24:36; John 20:19), "Do not be afraid" (Matthew 28:10), etc. Jesus knows that his disciples will be aghast at his appearance, having had their hopes destroyed just a short time earlier when he was crucified.

Reflection

The terms "fear not" and "do not be afraid" occur over fifty times in Scripture. This theme is also the dominant message of the risen Lord. While fear can be a healthy caution, it can be debilitating as well. The Lord who overcomes death is the same one who assures us that he will be with us. No matter what the future may hold, we will not have to face it alone.

To Think About

Always do what you are afraid to do.
(R. Waldo Emerson)

Prayer

Lord, since you are beside me, I will not fear. Amen.

Mary of Magdala went and announced to the disciples, "I have seen the Lord." (John 20:18)

April

14

Background
The Synoptic Gospels indicate that the disciples do not believe Mary's report. The fact that women are held in such low esteem within the culture makes it unlikely that a woman should be the one to bring such news—hence the reason for doubt. In this mission, however, Mary of Magdala becomes an example of what every Christian is called to be: a witness to the risen Christ based on personal experience rather than on someone else's testimony.

Reflection
The gospel accounts are set between two commands: "Come and see" (John 1:46) and "Go . . . and make" (Matthew 28:19). Once we have encountered Jesus, we are compelled to tell others. We find this again and again in the Gospels, the greatest instance being that of the Samaritan woman at the well (see John 4:4ff). Once she encounters Jesus, she runs to the village to tell others of her experience. We do well to ask ourselves, "Do others know that I have encountered Jesus by the way I live my life?"

To Think About
Nobody can experience Christ for me.

Prayer
Lord, may your light shine within me. Amen.

April

15

*With that their eyes were opened and they
recognized him. . . . (Luke 24:31a)*

Background
The verb for "were opened" occurs eight times in the
New Testament, and it always signifies a deeper
understanding of what is being revealed. Here we
find the disciples encountering Jesus at one level
and then, as they share a journey, conversation, a
meal and, above all, a little bit of hope, they come to
see their guest in a completely different light.

Reflection
A Prayer master asked his pupils when they might
know that it was dawn. Many answers were offered:
"When one is able to differentiate between a tree
and a cow." "When one can tell the difference
between an oak tree and a palm tree." The master
thanked his students but said that their answers
were not the one he was looking for. Finally, the students put the question to the master and he replied:
"When you can look into the face of a stranger and
see in it your brother, then it will be dawn; otherwise it will always be night."

To Think About
A stranger is but a friend that you have yet to make.

Prayer
Lord, grant me a trusting spirit and a forgiving
heart. Amen.

Jesus . . . stood in their midst and said, "Peace be with you." (John 20:26)

April 16

Background

The disciples, including the two who have returned from Emmaus, are gathered when Jesus enters into their midst. Luke emphasizes the difficulty the disciples have in accepting the miracle of the resurrection, despite the fact that many, including the women (see Luke 24:4-11), have shared their testimonies about seeing the risen Lord. The fact that Jesus suddenly appears, although the doors are shut, helps explain the surprise the disciples experience.

Reflection

True peace will be experienced only when our relations are as they should be—our relationship with God, our neighbor, and ourselves. When any one of these relationships is not what it should be, a state of inner anxiety results. It may be that there is someone or something preventing us from accepting the gift Jesus comes to give—the gift of inner peace.

To Think About

Peace is indivisible. (M. Litvinov)

Prayer

Lord, may I always strive for the peace of a quiet conscience. Amen.

April

17

Jesus said to them, "Come, have breakfast."
(John 21:12a)

Background
While some commentators point to this episode to illustrate how the risen Jesus shows the same tenderness he characterized in his public ministry, the primary aim of the story is to emphasize the reality of the resurrection. This Jesus is not some figment of the human imagination, and he isn't an ethereal disembodied spirit. Rather, he is Jesus, who suffered death and has risen.

Reflection
Not only is the way to a man's heart through his stomach, it is also the easiest way to his soul. Before we can speak to people about the love of Jesus, we must first feed them. While it may be humorous to say that "not on the word of God alone does man live," there is an element of truth to the statement. When people experience the touch of human kindness, they have little difficulty making the connection with Christ.

To Think About
It's good food and not fine words that keeps me alive. (Moliere)

Prayer
Lord, may I feel for others to the point of acting on their behalf. Amen.

"Go into the whole world and proclaim the gospel to every creature." (Mark 16:15)

April

18

Background
It is generally believed that Mark's Gospel actually concluded at verse 8 of this chapter, and that this passage is a summary appended to the Gospel. It gives a picture of what the early Christians believed the Church was meant to do and to be. They interpreted the mission of the Church to be a universal one, whereby they, as Church, were to be sent to the whole world in order to preach the gospel.

Reflection
The word of God is ever ancient and yet ever new. We often find it difficult to accept the fact, however, that it was written with a personal message for us today. So often we think that its commands are intended for those in ministry, those who have a vocation to preach. This day, we may touch people who have never heard of Jesus or been to a church. It may be the only opportunity they ever have to experience the Good News. Will it be a wasted opportunity?

To Think About
Preach not because you have to say something, but because you have something to say. (R.Whately)

Prayer
Lord, may my actions speak louder than my words. Amen.

April

19

"As the Father has sent me, so I send you."
(John 20:21)

Background

When he is about to ascend into heaven, Jesus sends his apostles to perpetuate the mission he himself has been given by the Father. Here we find Jesus transferring his own mission to the apostles. Through the apostles, this mission has been handed down to the pope and bishops who are the apostles' direct successors.

Reflection

Scripture tells us that Love prompted the Father to send the Son (see John 3:16). It is in this same love that we are sent; we are called by Love to bring a message of love to others. In the evening of our lives, we will be judged on how we have fulfilled this mission—on how well or how poorly we have loved.

To Think About

"I chose you." (John 15:16)

Prayer

Lord, may your love go before me this day so that love may meet love. Amen.

"No one can see the kingdom of God without being born from above." *(John 3:3)*

April

20

Background
The Jews think that a part of their very birthright is to enter the kingdom of God. In his comments to Nicodemus, however, Jesus says that this is not the case. Membership in the kingdom of God has little to do with the circumstances of our birth. Rather, to belong to the kingdom, we have to be born again by water and the Holy Spirit.

Reflection
Two people can view a work of art, and one may regard it as junk while the other considers it a masterpiece. The difference arises from the way we look at something. A trained and cultured eye will see things differently than an eye that is untrained and uncultured. Likewise, if God's Spirit is the driving force in our lives, everything will speak of the presence of God.

To Think About
To the beautiful, all things are beautiful.

Prayer
Lord, open the eyes of my heart to recognize you in the little events of my day. Amen.

April

21

"... so that everyone who believes in him may have eternal life." (John 3:15)

Background

Believing in Jesus necessitates an acceptance of the fact that God is as Jesus portrayed him. It implies that Jesus is the Son of God and, therefore, knows the mind of God. This obliges us to obey what Jesus asks of us and, if we do so, we will experience eternal life. This eternal life is not something we will have to await until the moment of death, but is one that can begin right now.

Reflection

There is all the difference in the world between "knowing" and "knowing about" someone. We can have a degree in theology and yet be an atheist. We can know far more about God than others know but not have the relationship with him that a person who is illiterate might have. "Knowing" someone, as distinct from "knowing about" that person, leads us from trusting to entrusting, from acceptance to commitment.

To Think About

God's greatness is only limited by my lack of commitment to him.

Prayer

Lord, let faith be my guide. Amen.

God so loved the world that he gave his only
Son. . . . (John 3:16)

April

22

Background
The simple love of God lies behind the whole plan of
salvation. Although the world was alienated from
God because of sin, this did not mean that the world
was evil in itself. Genesis reminds us that everything
that is created by God is good. It does, however,
emphasize the gratuity of God's love for the world
and the extent to which he is prepared to go in order
to show us this great love. It is a love that brings God
to the point of sacrificing his only Son.

Reflection
Many Christians are accused of being "Pelagian" in
the way they live their lives, i.e., they attempt to save
themselves by doing good works. We cannot and
need not save ourselves, however; Jesus Christ has
already achieved salvation for us. All we need do is
accept this salvation as the free gift that it is and
learn to live like people who are saved.

To Think About
The task of the Christian is to remind the world that
it is already saved.

Prayer
Lord, may your love for me inspire me to love you
above all else. Amen.

April

23

... whoever disobeys the Son will not see life....
(John 3:36)

Background
Some commentators see this verse reflecting the
challenge that is issued again and again throughout
history: the choice that is given to the Israelites in
Deuteronomy (see 30:15ff), where they are asked to
choose between life and death. We find it presented
once again in Joshua (see 24:15), where the choice is
given to serve or not to serve. What is important is
our response to Jesus Christ. If we opt for him, we
will know life. If sin is our priority, then there will not
be punishment but rather the consequences of sin.

Reflection
Obedience is the cornerstone of discipleship. When
we examine the word "obedience," we find that it
comes from the Latin phrase, *ab audiere,* which
means "from hearing." To be disciples presupposes
that we have learned to listen. Unless we listen to
God as he speaks through the circumstances of our
lives, through people, and in those moments of
silence, we cannot hope to learn obedience.

To Think About
If I learn to do what God asks, I should expect the
miracles that will follow.

Prayer
Speak, Lord, your servant is listening. Amen.

"There is a boy here who has five barley loaves and two fish; but what good are these for so many?" (John 6:9)

Background

The loaves that the boy has are made of barley, which is the food of the poor or the food of beasts. The fish are no more than sardines that swarm the Sea of Galilee. Hoping to have fresh fish on an occasion like this is out of the question. In such a warm climate there is no way of keeping fish refrigerated. In all probability the fish are pickled to keep them in an edible condition.

Reflection

The needs of our world are vast, and scarcely a day passes without some reminder about the great needs that others experience. When we think of the talents we have, we find they are puny compared to the needs of our world. However, if we are prepared to put our talents at God's disposal, God will make something beautiful of them. It is a fact that God still uses the lowly to confound the strong.

To Think About

Our world has yet to see what God can do with a life that is fully committed to him.

Prayer

Lord, I give you the five loaves and two fish of my life. Amen.

April

25

"A little while and you will no longer see me, and again a little while later and you will see me."
(John 16:16)

Background

Jesus' comment about two times—"a little while" and "again a little while later"—refers to the present and the future and is a concept that runs deep within Jewish thought. The Jews see the present time as something that is evil, a period that is under the condemnation of God. They see the time to come as being God's time and, consequently, a time of great blessings. Jesus' pending death and resurrection must be seen against the backdrop of this concept of time.

Reflection

Our journey through life is not a straight ascending line to total union with God. Rather, there are times when God appears to play hide-and-seek with us. What is important is that we realize that God never abandons us. We really don't need faith when things are going well for us, because we can see God at work within our lives. We certainly need faith, however, when things aren't going well!

To Think About

Just because it happens to be overcast doesn't mean that the sun is not shining.

Prayer

Lord, may I never let go of you. Amen.

"Follow me." *(John 21:19b)*

April

26

Background
Peter denies Jesus three times and now makes a threefold profession of his love for Jesus. When we love, there is always a price to pay. Peter will pay the ultimate price: his life. Because Jesus does not mince words in telling Peter about what is involved in following him, Peter is prepared to pay the cost of discipleship.

Reflection
No two words have changed the lives of people more than "follow me." At one time or another, every Christian hears those words. To answer with an undivided "yes" necessitates being prepared to leave everything. If we can appreciate the fruits that will flow from following Jesus, there will be only one response.

To Think About
I am most fulfilled when I live as Jesus wants me to.

Prayer
Lord, may I prize nothing above you. Amen.

April
27

"Do not work for food that perishes . . . but for the food that endures for eternal life." (John 6:27)

Background

Jesus reminds his listeners of the reason they are there: They witnessed the miracle of the multiplication of the loaves. The people are looking for the spectacular, whereas Jesus wants to satisfy an even deeper hunger: the hunger of the soul. Jesus accepts people where they are but is not satisfied to leave them there. Here again we find Jesus trying to lead his listeners to something higher, something of more lasting value.

Reflection

When we eat food it becomes a part of us by the process of digestion. When we receive holy Communion, however, we become a part of the one we receive; we become other Christs. When we receive holy Communion, we can in truth proclaim with Saint Paul: "Yet I live, no longer I, but Christ lives in me" (Galatians 2:20).

To Think About

"Whoever eats my flesh and drinks my blood remains in me." (John 6:54)

Prayer

Thank you, Lord, for entrusting yourself to me. Amen.

"I am the bread of life." (John 6:35)

April

28

Background
Jesus identifies himself with bread, the very
sustenance of life. The bread he speaks of, however,
is something more than mere "human" bread. Jesus
promises that he can satisfy the longings and
desires of the human heart with a "bread" that is the
very substance of life.

Reflection
The concept of canned food originated as food that
was cooked and bottled to feed the French army
when it was on the march. Christians are called a
pilgrim people and, on our march through life, we
are given the body and blood of Christ as our main-
stay. Regular reception will enable us to realize who
we are and to whom we belong. As the old German
proverb puts it: "Whose bread I eat, his song I sing."

To Think About
Since God is supplying the bread, I ought to think
about supplying the butter.

Prayer
Lord, may I hunger for you physically, emotionally,
and spiritually. Amen.

April 29

"I will not reject anyone who comes to me."
(John 6:37)

Background
Jesus comes to do the will of the Father by doing the Father's work. The Father's will is that all of us, his children, be saved through being gathered into his kingdom. Jesus has won salvation for us and that salvation is offered to us regardless of our unworthiness. Each one of us, however, has to make the choice to accept or reject Jesus.

Reflection
When Charles Dickens was asked what was, in his opinion, the greatest short story ever written, he replied: "The Prodigal Son." The story depicts the Father as someone who is constantly waiting for the return of the wayward, penitent child. Jesus is the image of the Father and he, too, awaits those who are lost. It's never too late to turn around and begin our return journey to our waiting God.

To Think About
It is better to begin in the evening than not at all.
(English proverb)

Prayer
Lord, may I never doubt your love for me. Amen.

"No one can come to me unless the Father who sent me draw him." (John 6:44)

April

30

Background
The Greek word for draw is *helkuein,* and its meaning implies "a resistance." This is the word used to describe how Paul and Silas are dragged before the magistrates in Philippi (see Acts 16:19). It is also the word used to explain how Peter "dragged the net ashore full of one hundred and fifty-three large fish" (John 21:11).

Reflection
The greatest gift we can receive, after the gift of life, is the gift of baptism. From the moment we receive this gift, the Spirit works quietly within us, praying to the Father (see Romans 8:26). As with all growth, it can take years before the workings of the Spirit are evident in our lives. Perhaps slowly but most surely, the Holy Spirit—God's seal of ownership on us—will lead us through Jesus to the Father.

To Think About
I am a child of God.

Prayer
May I never forget the dignity of my calling. Amen.

May

1

"Whoever eats my flesh and drinks my blood has eternal life." *(John 6:54)*

Background
According to Jesus, the guarantee of the resurrection of the body is the eating and drinking of his body and blood. While this concept may be difficult for us today, it would have been relatively easy for a person brought up within the context of ancient sacrifice, where an animal that had been sacrificed was seldom burned in its entirety. In such a culture, only a small piece of the animal would have been burned as a sacrificial token; then some meat would have been given to the priest and the remainder would have been eaten by family and friends of the person who had made the sacrifice. God was deemed to have entered the sacrifice once it had been offered.

Reflection
Eternal life is not something promised as the reward of a life well spent or sacrifices offered; rather, it is a gift that is offered here and now. As such, it cannot be explained; it can only be received and experienced.

To Think About
Many of us wonder about life after death, and few of us wonder about life before death.

Prayer
Lord, slow me down so that I may enjoy life. Amen.

. . . many [of] his disciples returned to their former way of life and no longer accompanied him. (John 6:66)

Background

In John 6:52, we read that the promise of the Eucharist is the cause of arguments among those who heard Christ at Capernaum. Some are so scandalized that they decide to no longer follow Jesus. This rejection is just a sample of the Jews' eventual rejection of Jesus and his ministry that is to follow (see John. 21:37ff).

Reflection

Time and again we read or hear about people who have endured situations that appear to be unbearable. The martyrs are examples of such people. The reason these people manage to suffer so heroically is because they have an invincible relationship with Christ. The German philosopher Nietzsche put it rather succinctly when he wrote that the one who has a "why" (purpose) can endure almost any "how" (circumstances).

To Think About

What is my "why" and what is my "how"?

Prayer

Lord, together we are invincible; apart from you I am nothing. Amen.

"I give them eternal life." (John 10:28a)

Background

Many times in the pages of the New Testament we find Jesus comparing himself to a shepherd. Shepherds in the Holy Land can call each of their sheep by name and the sheep will respond to their shepherd, whose voice they know. To say that the sheep are dependent on their shepherds would be an understatement, for sheep depend on shepherds for the very sustenance of life itself.

Reflection

Thomas Carlyle, the Scottish essayist and historian, told us that the person who does not have an understanding of eternity will never get a true hold of time. For many, eternity or eternal life is something that only begins when one dies. This is not so; it begins now. Jesus himself explains that eternal life is to be in a living relationship with the Father and Jesus, whom he sent.

To Think About

Time is but a human effort to organize eternity.

Prayer

Lord, keep my feet on the ground and my eyes focused on heaven. Amen.

"I came that they might have life and have it more abundantly." *(John 10:10)*

Background
For John the Evangelist, everything, even inanimate objects, has life, and this life means more than mere existence. It signifies a sharing in the being of God. It is a life of ultimate understanding, the revelation of God. The Greek word *pleroma,* meaning "having it more abundantly," implies having life to the greatest possible degree—having the fullest possible experience of life.

Reflection
Jesus comes to offer eternal life to those who long for it; he does not force it on anyone. We all know that it is impossible to place something in a fist that is shut tightly. This is true of life; we are free to accept or refuse Jesus' offer. We can hold the fists of life wide open, ready to receive, or we can clench our fists tightly shut and refuse the gift. The decision to accept what Jesus wants to give us, however, will necessitate changes.

To Think About
To be able to distinguish between the important and the urgent in life is a precious gift.

Prayer
Lord, may I be willing to sacrifice the lesser for the greater. Amen.

May

5

"The Father and I are one." (John 10:30)

Background

Jesus does not say that he and the Father are merely "in communion" or that he and God are "as one." No, the Greek word used is *hen,* which means that he and his Father are "one and the same," an expression that is especially difficult for the Jews to accept. This unity is founded on the perfect love of Jesus for the Father and his obedience to what his Father asks of him.

Reflection

Because Jesus is completely one with the Father, he can claim that everything he says and does is directed by the Father (see John 14:10). What a beautiful example and model for living the Christian way of life. To the extent that we are in touch with Jesus, through prayer and the sacraments, we will find that everything we do and say will be according to the mind of God. What more could we ask for?

To Think About

Acting for others presupposes that we know them.

Prayer

Father, may my life reflect your desires for me. Amen.

"I did not come to condemn the world but to save the world." (John 12:47)

Background
God loves the world so much that he sends his only Son. Jesus does not come into the world, however, as an expression of God's anger or wrath; rather, Jesus is as an expression of God's love. We will be judged on how we respond to this expression of love. If we accept Jesus' love, we will be saved; if we choose not to accept that love, we will be lost.

Reflection
As Christians, it is our privilege to serve those we meet. Genuine service presupposes love and love does not condemn, for to God alone belongs the right to judge and condemn. When we find that life becomes a clearer reflection of the gospel, we will find that judgment and condemnation begin to fade.

To Think About
Before I condemn, it might be wise for me to pause to judge the one who is judging!

Prayer
Lord, may I learn to love more and to judge less. Amen.

May

7

"Whoever receives the one I send receives me, and whoever receives me receives the one who sent me." *(John 13:20)*

Background
Here we find the identification of the disciples with Jesus; he is encountered in those who proclaim his gospel. Jesus is emphasizing the relationship between slave and master, and between messenger and the one who sends the messenger. In other words, Jesus is assuring his disciples that the one who is prepared to identify with him will be identified with the one who sent him.

Reflection
God comes into our lives in the most unexpected situations and at the most unexpected times. While we may sometimes find it difficult to recognize his presence, we can be sure that whenever we experience love, we experience God, for God is Love (see 1 John 4:8). We need to have our antennae finely tuned if we are to recognize the many ways, even within a day, that Love approaches us.

To Think About
Love is a decision that leads one to a joyful heart.

Prayer
Lord, grant me a joyful, loving heart. Amen.

"Do not let your hearts be troubled."
(John 14:1)

Background

Jesus has been talking to his little group of disciples about having to leave them. He realizes that they are heavy of heart because everything they had hoped for is being destroyed. Into all of this, he speaks these reassuring words, exhorting his disciples to trust in the Father and in him.

Reflection

There are two days we can do little about. The first is yesterday; it's gone. All we can hope to do about yesterday is learn from its experiences. The other day is tomorrow, which has yet to come. By using the opportunities provided today, we make the best possible preparations for meeting tomorrow—never forgetting that God is already there.

To Think About

Trouble is but another name for opportunity finely disguised.

Prayer

Lord, may I appreciate that you are a God of the "now." Amen.

May

9

"If you ask anything of me in my name, I will do it." (John 14:14)

Background

This is the only verse in John's Gospel that mentions prayer as being addressed to Jesus personally rather than to the Father through Jesus. The conditions for the effectiveness of prayer are stated beginning with verse 16: love and obedience. Prayer that is prayed in the name of Jesus and that asks for his will to be done is always answered.

Reflection

Petitionary prayer is an area of prayer that presents problems for so many people. How often we ask for something we know to be good, only to find that our prayer goes unanswered—at least that's the way it seems! But time has its own work to do. One day we may realize that our "unanswered prayer" has been answered in a way we never expected and in a way that surpasses even our wildest expectations.

To Think About

God will give me only what is good for me.

Prayer

Thank you, Father, for all your gifts. Amen.

"This is how all will know that you are my disciples, if you have love one for another."
(John 13:35)

May
10

Background
In the Book of Leviticus (see 19:18), we are commanded to love our neighbor. Jesus underlines this point by saying that it contains the kernel of the whole Law, along with the love of God. He gives it a new depth, however, by explaining that his disciples should love one another—just as he loves us.

Reflection
There is an old Russian proverb that says, "Love is a glass which shatters if you hold it too tightly or too loosely." Learning to love can be a long and difficult process. The difficulty arises in allowing those we love to have the freedom to be themselves, to become the people God wants them to be.

To Think About
Kindness is the golden chain by which society is bound together. (J. Goethe)

Prayer
Lord, may I build bridges in preference to erecting walls. Amen.

"Whoever has my commandments and observes them is the one who loves me." *(John 14:21)*

Background

Love is one of the underlying themes of John's Gospel—the love between the Father and Jesus, the love of Jesus for his disciples, and the love disciples must have for the Father, for Jesus, and for one another. The acid test of any love is the obedience that is shown to what is asked. It is obedience that is the precondition for God revealing himself.

Reflection

If Jesus wanted half-hearted disciples, he would have interspersed his preaching with "ifs" and "buts." He didn't! His teachings are, by and large, clear and concise, and his gauge for testing our love is the simple keeping of his commandments. It is the same measure as his love for the Father. Could anything be more straightforward?

To Think About

God's commandments draw me closer to everlasting life.

Prayer

Bend my heart to your will, O God. Amen.

"Do not let your hearts be troubled or afraid."
(John 14:27)

Background
The heart can be untroubled only when peace is present. The concept of "peace," or "shalom," as used in the Bible, however, means much more than the absence of struggle or strife. Peace is the ability to deal with those things that underlie the concept of peace. Peace is less a "freedom from" strife and more a "freedom for" dealing with strife when it arises.

Reflection
Time and again the Gospels present us with examples of how the presence of Jesus in a situation brings peace and calm. Indeed, the presence of another person can often act as a source of strength and consolation when we find ourselves in difficult situations. If we invite Jesus into each of our days, our lives will not necessarily have less trouble; they will, however, have much less fear.

To Think About
Whatever the situation, I know that Jesus is there in the moment with me.

Prayer
Lord, with you by my side I am invincible. Amen.

May

13

"Without me you can do nothing." (John 15:5)

Background
Jesus is telling his disciples that it isn't sufficient to
be an Israelite in order to belong to God; rather, his
disciples can hope to find their way to God's salvation only by attachment to him, the Son of God.

Reflection
Many Christians are of the opinion that when everything else fails, try Jesus. So often we "go it alone"
and wonder why our lives are so barren, so empty.
Jesus comes to offer us life (see John 10:10), and it's
only when we accept the complete package he offers
that we will come to experience a life within life.

To Think About
Is Jesus my first or my last resort?

Prayer
In you alone, O Lord, rests my salvation. I turn to
you for life within life. Amen.

"It was not you who chose me, but I who chose you and appointed you to go and bear fruit that will remain." (John 15:16)

Background

Throughout history, the story of salvation has always been one of God taking the initiative. As John reminds us, it is God who so loves the world that he sends his only Son. We find this same initiative in Jesus, who chooses us to be his disciples. Why we were chosen is something we will never know. With being chosen, however, comes a responsibility—to bear fruit that will rebound to the glory of God.

Reflection

The bombing of World War II destroyed a village in the south of Germany, including its church. When the people searched through the rubble, they came across the statue of the Sacred Heart. Amazingly, it had incurred little damage, except its hands were missing. When the war ended, the people repaired their church and intended to repair the statute. Instead, the statue was placed back on its stand, minus the hands, with the inscription: "I have no other hands to work with but yours, no other tongue to speak with but yours."

To Think About

To bury my talent is a grave mistake.

Prayer

Lord, take what's mine and make it thine. Amen.

May

14

May 15

"No one has greater love than this, to lay down one's life for one's friends." (John 15:13)

Background

Love is the law of the Old Testament, a point brought out in Leviticus 19:18. Christ widens the understanding of the law of love, however, to include not just one's friends but all of humankind. Christ's love, shown by the laying down of his life for us, is the model we must follow and the motive we must embrace.

Reflection

As Christians, our basic vocation is to incarnate the love of Jesus. It's a calling to put the needs of others before our own—and this is easier said than done! The contradiction in Christianity, however, is that the extent to which we are prepared to let go of our lives for others is, in fact, the extent to which we will find life. We will experience happiness ourselves to the extent that we strive to make others happy.

To Think About

The greatest use I can make of life is to spend it for others and for Christ.

Prayer

Lord, may I learn to give to others and to you without counting the cost. Amen.

" . . . I have chosen you out of the world . . ."
(John 15:19b)

Background
For John the Evangelist, the kingdom of the world is
directly opposed to the kingdom of God; there can
never be any sense of compromise between the two.
Being chosen from the world means persecution. At
the time John writes, being known as a Christian is
sufficient cause for execution.

Reflection
Knowing that Jesus chooses us for a mission, where
we are to fulfil that mission doesn't really matter.
Even in the face of rejection and persecution, we go
where our call leads, for we have been chosen "out of
the world" to build the kingdom of God.

To Think About
The calling of every man and woman is to serve
other people. (L. Tolstoy)

Prayer
Lord, may I never forget how much you depend on
me and I on you. Amen.

"... and we will come to him and make our dwelling with him." (John 14:23b)

Background

Jesus' promise to dwell within his followers can be seen as a progression of God's proclamation in the Old Testament that he will dwell among his people (see Exodus 29:45; Ezekiel 37:26-27). Two conditions have to be met for this to happen, however. First, there has to be love; second there has to be obedience, which is the expression of love.

Reflection

The longest and most difficult journey that we must undertake is the journey to our center. When we are prepared to make the journey, loneliness will no longer feature as one of our world's greatest problems. The first and most important part of that journey is, as Jesus tells us, the living of our lives according to his word.

To Think About

Your daily life is your temple and your religion. (K. Gibran)

Prayer

May your word be a guide for my path. Amen.

"The hour is coming when everyone who kills you will think he is offering worship to God."
(John 16:2)

Background
In the Hebrew exposition of the Scriptures, the one who sheds the blood of the godless is seen in the same vein as the one who offers sacrifice (see Numbers 25:13). Misguided persecutors often feel, in all sincerity, that they are serving God by calling to task those of other religious persuasions. A prime example of this is Paul prior to his conversion to Christianity.

Reflection
Christianity will always have its price and, quite often, the price is rejection by others! Unless our living of the Christian way of life involves suffering, we should ask if what we profess is, in fact, Christianity. Christianity without the cross is a contradiction in terms. Not all rejection need necessarily be bad!

To Think About
To remove the cross from Christianity is like removing oxygen from breathing.

Prayer
May I be found worthy to suffer for you, O Lord. Amen.

May
18

"But if I go, I will send him [the Advocate] to you." (John 16:7)

Background

For John, the era of the Church is the era of the Spirit. While Christ is on earth, there has not as yet been a complete outpouring of the Spirit. This is to be one of the consequences of the glorification of Christ. Part of the mission of the glorified Christ is to send the Spirit from the Father to prolong and bring to completion the work begun by him, the work being carried on by his Church.

Reflection

Jews believe that when the spirit, or *ruach,* leaves a person, the person is dead. When we stop to think about it, there is nothing more deadly than a person or a group without a spirit. How often we find ourselves within a group where we feel like saying: "Let's join hands to see if we can contact the living!" It is no less a power than the Spirit of God that is available to us if only we are prepared to give him free reign.

To Think About

What changes would occur if God's Spirit were given free reign in my life?

Prayer

Come, Holy Spirit, and enkindle within me the power of your love. Amen.

"Everything the Father has is mine."
(John 16:15)

May

20

Background
Although the precise doctrine of the Blessed Trinity
was not fully formulated until much later, we find it
coming through again and again in the Gospels.
Here Jesus is attesting to the fact that everything the
Father has belongs to him. It speaks of the unity of
mind and heart that underpins everything Jesus
does.

Reflection
A story is told of three young people who were each
given the opportunity to fill a shopping cart with
whatever they wanted to collect from the store
within five minutes. Two of the young people dashed
around, up and down the aisles, filling their carts,
while the third simply ambled at a leisurely pace.
When asked afterwards why she had been so slow,
she replied: "Why should I rush? My father owns the
store."

To Think About
My Father is the creator of heaven and earth. He
owns the lot!

Prayer
Lord, thank you for your bountiful gifts. Amen.

May

21

"... *they were continually in the temple praising God.*" *(Luke 24:53b)*

Background

Luke's Gospel finishes where it begins—in the Temple. While we may view the Ascension as the end of an epoch, it is also correct to see it as a new beginning. Jesus, having accomplished his mission, passes the baton, so to speak, to his disciples; he has finished his work and ours is just beginning. We do have the promise, however, that we are not alone in our efforts.

Reflection

To praise God is among the greatest acts of faith that a human being can make. When we praise God, we acknowledge that he is working all things for the best, even if the results appear otherwise. To "allow" God to be God is one of the most difficult demands that can be made on us; so often we want God to be reasonable, to do things our way.

To Think About

It is the glory of man to continue and remain in the service of God. (Saint Irenaeus)

Prayer

Lord, may I praise you for what I can understand and trust you for what I cannot. Amen.

"... your grief will become joy ... and no one will take your joy away from you." *(John 16:20.22)*

May

22

Background
Jesus assures his disciples that the grief they are experiencing because he is about to leave them will only be temporary. He will return and their sorrow will be transformed into joy. He continues to assure them that this joy will be lasting, and cannot be taken from them.

Reflection
Saying "yes" to Jesus will always have its price. At times we may be inclined to wonder if it's worth the effort or pain. From experience, we know that there is no joy like the joy we realize in the giving of our best for Jesus; it's just one of the many fruits of happiness. This is the joy that no money can buy, although the price we have to pay is often high.

To Think About
The most useless day of all is that in which we have not laughed. (S. Chamfort)

Prayer
Lord, where there is sadness, let me bring joy. Amen.

"Ask and you will receive."
(John 16:24)

Background

Because Jesus Christ is our intercessor in heaven, we are assured that we will receive whatever we ask for in his name. Asking in his name, however, necessitates that we know what we are asking. Our prayer will be answered only if it is for our good. Because he is our Savior, Jesus will not grant us what we ask unless he knows that it is for our good.

Reflection

There's a beautiful story told of a little boy who prayed for a bicycle for his birthday. His parents were heartbroken because there was no way they could afford such a gift. On the morning of the little boy's birthday, his parents were surprised to find their son content, although he didn't get the bicycle he wanted. "Are you not angry with God for not having heard your prayer?" they asked. "Ah! but he did," explained the boy, "and he said 'no.'"

To Think About

God alone knows my needs and what's best for me.

Prayer

Lord, you have brought me safely to this point of my journey. Let me trust you for the rest. Amen.

"... so that they all may be one, as you, Father, are in me and I in you." (John 17:21)

May

24

Background
Part of our human nature inclines us to pull apart rather than to unite. This is vividly portrayed in the account of the tower of Babel (see Genesis 11:9) and in the wars and rumors of wars that have been so much a part of recorded history. The unity that Jesus prays for between his disciples is a unity of hearts, a unity of personal relationships.

Reflection
Unity, whether it be political or religious, may appear beyond anything we can accomplish. We think, "If only I were the pope" or "If only I were the president"—perhaps then we'd have a greater hope of achieving unity. We can achieve unity, however, where people like the pope and the president cannot. We can work toward establishing unity within and among ourselves, at home, in the work place, and within the various groups to which we belong.

To Think About
Unless I'm bringing unity among those with whom I live, I'm probably causing disunity.

Prayer
Lord, may I leave the imprint of your love on every heart that I touch this day. Amen.

May 25

"In the world you will have trouble, but take courage, I have conquered the world."
(John 16:33)

Background

Within a short time Jesus is going to confront and overcome the cross on Calvary. The disciples realize that they, too, will be confronted with persecution. In this farewell discourse, Jesus assures his disciples that his victory will also belong to them and they need only have courage. Jesus' followers can achieve what Jesus achieves.

Reflection

A story is told of a child who strayed into the devil's storeroom where he found all the seeds that the devil plants within people's hearts. The child noticed that the largest of all the barrels was marked "discouragement." When the child inquired why this was so, he was told that these were the seeds that took root most quickly. The child then asked if those seeds grew everywhere, to which the devil replied: "No, we cannot get them to grow in hearts that are thankful, no matter how hard we try!"

To Think About

What's brave, what's noble, let's do it.
(W. Shakespeare)

Prayer

Lord, grant me a thankful heart. Amen.

"... and I have been glorified in them."
(John 17:10)

Background
Although the disciples have already glorified Jesus through their fidelity, Jesus is presumably referring to the glory he will receive through their future works on his behalf. As with the human body, the head will share in both the pleasure and the suffering that the rest of the body experiences.

Reflection
It often seems that it would be easy to become a saint if we only lived in a different place or in different age. Yet, we are called to be saints right where we are—in the daily circumstances of our lives. God has given us just the right ingredients we need to be saints; we simply fail to appreciate this. If the gospel is to be preached in our own corner of the globe, it will depend on each of us, individually, responding to God's call to sainthood in our own place and time.

To Think About
My sainthood rests in my ordinary life.

Prayer
Lord, may no effort be too great and may no task be too small. Amen.

"I do not ask that you take them out of the world but that you keep them from the evil one. . . ."
(John 17:15)

Background

The term "world" is sometimes used by John to mean God's enemy, the evil one's kingdom. In this sense, the world is something opposed to Christ and his followers (see John 1:10). In this passage, Jesus states that he and his disciples do not belong to the world. Although his disciples may have to live "in" this world, he prays that they will not "be of" this world and that they will be protected from the evil one to whom the world belongs.

Reflection

We all know the desire of wanting to protect those we love. Jesus knows that he cannot be with his disciples always, and so he entrusts them to the Father's protection. In the same way, our loved ones are not ours; they are "on loan" to us. By giving them to the Father, we rid ourselves of a heavy burden and place it where it belongs—in the Father's arms!

To Think About

God couldn't be everywhere so he created you and me.

Prayer

Lord, I ask you to protect those who are your gifts of love to me. Amen.

". . . that they all may be one, . . . that the world may believe that you sent me." (John 17:21)

May
28

Background
In this prayer, Jesus is asking that his disciples display evidence of loving unity so that his mission might be effective. It is this unity that will convince the world that the disciples are sent by Jesus, just as Jesus is sent by the Father. Only this unity will convince the world that the Father's love can be seen in his disciples, as it was evident in Jesus himself.

Reflection
The Romans have a tactic in battle that never fails; it is called "divide and conquer." They try to separate the opposing army into splinter groups and thus gain a strategic advantage. From this arose the saying: "United we stand, divided we fall." As Jesus' followers, we form a part of his mystical body, and the well-being of the whole body depends on the well-being of each member.

To Think About
Our greatest achievements are those that benefit others.

Prayer
Lord, may I be open to you at work within my neighbor. Amen.

May

29

"*Do you love me? . . . Feed my sheep.*"
(*John 21:17, 19*)

Background

The Peter that we see in this scenario is a different Peter from the one we encounter in other parts of the Gospel. Instead of being the overconfident disciple we encounter in Matthew 26:33, this Peter humbly admits that Jesus knows all things, especially how much Peter loves him. It will be this love that will eventually cause Peter to follow Jesus to the point of laying down his life for him.

Reflection

Before we become disciples of Jesus we have to fall in love with him. For the one who loves, nothing is too great or too small. Every opportunity is used to express that love. The problem is not so much "falling in love" but "staying in love." As in human love, when the initial euphoria evaporates, the love must be expressed in the routine bits and pieces of each day.

To Think About

Feigned affection is worse than a curse.

Prayer

Lord, be my partner in the dance of life. Amen.

"You follow me." (John 21:22b)

May
30

Background

Throughout the Gospels Jesus repeatedly waives aside questions that are asked out of mere curiosity—and we find him doing that here. The important thing for Peter is not to be curious about what the future holds for the beloved disciple, John, but to serve the Lord by faithfully living out the calling he himself has received.

Reflection

The Gospels were written for us today. This invitation or command is given to us every bit as much as it is given to Peter in the Gospel. How it is lived will have to be worked out within the particular vocation to which we have been called. Saint Thérèse of Lisieux made this the hallmark of her sanctity. She discovered that love is at the heart of every vocation within the Church.

To Think About

The path to Christ leads through the present moment.

Prayer

Lord, guide me in the path that you would have me walk. Amen.

May
31

"No one who sets a hand to the plow and looks to what was left behind is fit for the kingdom of God." (Luke 9:62)

Background

As always, Jesus turns to his surroundings when he wishes to site an example to make a point. In Palestine at the time of Jesus, a plow is guided by one hand while the other hand drives the oxen. To plow a field, a person needs to be well skilled. If one looks back or away from the work at hand, for example, the furrow becomes crooked and the job is ruined.

Reflection

For Christians, there is no clear-cut path; there are only directives, and the path unfolds while walking the Christian way day by day. As we attempt to carve out our own path, we may find ourselves torn between what is good and what is best. We may even wonder if we have made a mistake in our choice of vocations, feeling like we could have served God in a better way had we made other choices. It is only love that determines the value of any life.

To Think About

To God alone belong the seed and the harvest.

Prayer

May you accomplish great works through my simple deeds. Amen.

"I have come not to abolish but to fulfill."
(Matthew 5:17)

Background
Time and again, Jesus drives the proverbial coach
and four through the Law. In fact, it is precisely
because he is a lawbreaker that he is condemned
and eventually executed. Here we find Jesus saying
that he hasn't come to abolish the Law but to fulfill
it. What Jesus rejects is that which has come to be
accepted as the Law—the Pharisaic interpretation
of it—rather than its original meaning.

Reflection
When we face a difficult situation, we may be
tempted to put it aside and begin fresh. In some
instances, this may be the only way to move forward. In most instances, however, we will find that
there is much good in what already exists, and that
the challenge is to take what is good and make it
better. This is how the Lord handles us when, having
fallen because of sin, we come before him.

To Think About
Today's greatest challenge is not to recycle used
materials but to reclaim in love those people who
have fallen.

Prayer
Lord, show me your beauty in each person, especially in those whom this world despises. Amen.

June

2

"Be patient with me, and I will pay you back in full." (Matthew 18:26)

Background
According to rabbinic teaching, forgiveness of a neighbor is normally limited to three times. When Peter tries to be magnanimous, he suggests that forgiveness should be given seven times. Seven has significance for the Jew; it signifies totality. Jesus, however, expands the number of times we should forgive to seven times seventy, indicating that there can be no measurable limit to forgiveness.

Reflection
The man who is in debt to the king for a sum almost impossible to repay simply asks for time. What he receives is a complete remission of his entire debt. In the same way, the extent of our forgiveness has to be total. An old Japanese saying tells us that forgiveness has to be similar to drawing pictures on water, inasmuch as the person has to be forgiven and the offense has to be forgotten.

To Think About
They who forgive most will be most forgiven.
(English proverb)

Prayer
Lord, heal the wounds of past offenses so that I may truly forgive. Amen.

"Therefore, I say to you, the kingdom of God will be taken away from you and given to a people that will produce its fruit." (Matthew 21:43)

Background
In Palestine at the time of Jesus, there are a lot of absentee landlords who let out their estates and remain interested in only the money that can be made. Payment is usually made in one of three ways: a monetary rent, a fixed amount of fruit, or a fixed percentage of the crop the estate produces. On the part of the landlords, there is little concern for either the land or the tenants.

Reflection
We are told that the happiest people on earth are the saints, people who constantly say "yes" to God in what he asks of them. We are confronted with the same challenge of the Gospels that the saints faced, a challenge that is meted out to us many times each day. In learning to answer "yes" to what the Gospels ask of us, we come to a depth of happiness we never dreamed possible. We grow "stronger" as we answer "yes" to God.

To Think About
Each conception of spiritual beauty is a glimpse of God. (M. Mendelssohn)

Prayer
May I know the joy of answering "yes" to what you ask of me. Amen.

June

4

> "Can you drink the cup that I am going to drink?" *(Matthew 20:22)*

Background

Jesus was speaking to both James and John, but the cup that is offered does not have the same implications for each of them. James is the first of the apostles to die of martyrdom. John, however, according to tradition, lives in Ephesus to a ripe old age and dies of natural causes. The cup that we are asked to drink is everything that our vocation in life demands of us.

Reflection

An old Greek proverb assures us that the one who suffers much will know much. While we might not deliberately choose it, suffering can open our eyes to what really matters. When we are in pain, insignificant things fade into the background and we begin to realize that God is the only one who can help us. Suffering has been likened to the doorway to God's heart; it often drives us into his arms.

To Think About

That which is bitter to endure may be sweet to remember.

Prayer

Lord, thank you for your promise that you will never abandon me. Amen.

"Pray for those who persecute you."
(Matthew 5:44)

Background

Jesus knows the human condition better than any other person. He does not suggest that we pray for those who persecute us; rather, he commands it! Jesus knows that, like love, forgiveness is a decision. He knows that nobody can pray for another and still hate that person. He knows that the best way of curing bitterness is to pray for the person we are tempted to hate.

Reflection

Our mental attitudes normally govern our behavior. When we see others as enemies, it is often due to the way we think about them. Because we feel that they have committed a real or imaginary offense against us, we shut them out. When we pray for them, however, our attitude changes and we often mellow to the point where we come to see them in a more realistic way. Prayer often removes the blindfold from our eyes.

To Think About

Friendship is often a matter of perspective.

Prayer

Forgive me my offenses as I forgive those who have offended me. Amen.

He breathed on them and said to them, "Receive the holy Spirit." (John 20:22)

Background

It is rather interesting that John, in an effort to describe this new creation, uses the same verb as the Greek word used to describe the original creation in Genesis 2:7. While there may be a chronological discrepancy between the giving of the Spirit as recorded by Luke and the one here in John, what is being stressed is the intimate connection between the resurrection and the energizing of the Church by the Spirit.

Reflection

Jesus entrusts the task of continuing his work to the group as a whole, for the whole is strong, and to each individual, for the individual is a part of the whole. We are empowered by God's Spirit that is given to us through the family we call Church.

To Think About

A three-ply cord is not easily broken.
(Ecclesiastes 4:12)

Prayer

Come, Holy Spirit, strengthen and renew me with the power of your love. Amen.

". . . Do not worry about how you are to speak or what you are to say. You will be given at that moment what you are to say." (Matthew 10:19)

Background
This is part of Matthew's collection of Jesus' sayings about persecution. Jesus never leaves any of his listeners in doubt as to what awaits them if they decide to follow him. At that time—and perhaps not so different today—a Christian can expect persecution to come from the state, the established Church of the time, or even a family member.

Reflection
What makes us acceptable to others is not the accent with which we speak or the eloquence of the words we use. Rather, it is the person within that determines our words and our actions. If we focus on trying to make Jesus a part of each act we perform, our words and our actions will be marked by the authenticity of love. If our love is enduring, persecution will cease.

To Think About
Suit the action to the word, the word to the action. (W. Shakespeare)

Prayer
Lord, I know that you are listening. Amen.

June

7

June

8

"Many that are first will be last, and [the] last will be first." (Mark 10:31)

Background

The hidden meaning of these words is not lost on the Jews. They, who consider themselves to be over and above anyone and everyone, are destined to be the least of all and the last to be chosen. Those they consider "nobody" will be selected to be the first in the kingdom of God.

Reflection

Peter is headstrong and hot-tempered. Matthew is a tax collector and most probably a cheat. James and John are only concerned with their own welfare. Simon the Zealot belongs to an illegal organization. These are but a few examples of people—imperfect and weak human beings—whom Jesus uses to do great work. If he can use them, can he not also use us?

To Think About

We are the gloves and God's Spirit is the hand that empowers the gloves.

Prayer

Lord, transform my weakness with your strength. Amen.

"Teacher, we want you to do for us whatever we ask of you." (Mark 10:35)

June

9

Background
This episode shows the honesty of Mark. While Matthew's account tries to save some dignity for James and John by attributing the question to their mother, Mark names and shames the two disciples. It gives us an insight into the true characters of some of the early followers of Jesus. Like us, they are mere human beings who are driven by ambition and who fail to understand what Jesus is about.

Reflection
When will we realize that God knows what is best for us, that our happiness and his will are one and the same? As we grow closer to Jesus, we make our own that part of the Our Father that prays "Thy will be done." When his will is done, our lives can get no better.

To Think About
The future that we journey toward is in God's hands. Could it be in better hands?

Prayer
Lord, I want to do whatever you ask of me. Amen.

June

10

But he kept calling out all the more....
(Mark 10:48)

Background

Jesus is on his way to the Passover when this incident with the blind Bartimeus takes place. Whenever a learned rabbi is traveling, it is customary for him to be surrounded by disciples who listen to him discoursing as he walks along. Bartimeus, hearing the commotion of the passing crowd, is being persistent in his attempts to get near Jesus.

Reflection

In his autobiography, *Up From Slavery,* George Washington Carver describes how he was somewhat perplexed when he arrived to sit an entrance examination for Hampton Institute. He was asked to sweep the classroom. He swept it three times and dusted it four times. The headmaster brushed a ledge with his clean handkerchief and, when he could find no dust said: "I guess you will do to enter this institution." Carver achieved his goal by being persistent in his assigned responsibilities.

To Think About

If a task is once begun, never leave it until it's properly done.

Prayer

Lord, like the blind Bartimeus, may I never give up. Amen.

"When you stand to pray, forgive anyone against whom you have a grievance...." (Mark 11:25)

June
11

Background
In this passage, Jesus reminds us of our need to know what we are doing when we pray. It is difficult to go to God without going through our neighbor. In other words, we must forgive if we are to open the channel of communication between ourselves and God.

Reflection
Our relationship with God reflects the Trinity: Not only does it involve God and us, it also involves our neighbors. We cannot tell God that we love him until we've told our neighbors that we love them. We cannot ask God's forgiveness until we have asked for our neighbors' forgiveness. As with the image of the cross, whatever goes upward to God must also go outward to our neighbors.

To Think About
When I forgive, I set two people free: my enemy and myself.

Prayer
Lord, enable me to forget so that I can more easily forgive. Amen.

June

12

"Repay to Caesar what belongs to Caesar and to God what belongs to God." (Mark 12:17)

Background

In responding to the Pharisees who are trying to trap him, Jesus asks for a denarius, which bears the image of the reigning emperor, Tiberius Caesar. One of the first things that a conqueror did when he captured a territory was to issue his own coinage as a sign of his power in the land.

Reflection

A Catholic priest and a Protestant minister were discussing how they divided up their Sunday collections. The minister said that he draws a straight line on the ground and throws the contents of the collection plate into the air. That which lands on the right side of the line belongs to God and that which lands on the left side of the line he keeps for his own needs. The priest said that he does the same thing. We can so easily find reasons for giving "Caesar" far more than his share, whether it is in money or time!

To Think About

Those I work for may want my best. God, on the other hand, wants my all.

Prayer

Lord, today is your gift to me. What I make of it will become my gift to you. Amen.

"He is not God of the dead but of the living."
(Mark 12:27)

Background
The Sadducees look to the Pentateuch, the first five books of the Old Testament, for their beliefs. They insist that the Pentateuch offers no evidence for resurrection. On the other hand, the Pharisees believe in the resurrection, so when the question is put to Jesus about resurrection, it is actually a trap. Jesus answers by meeting them on their own ground when he quotes from Exodus 3:6.

Reflection
The saying goes: "A nod is as good as a wink to a blind horse." Similarly, for those who are blind to the workings of God in their lives, miracles never happen. For spiritual persons, on the other hand, the world is transfused with the glory of God; each event is silhouetted against the backdrop of God's loving concern. For such people, God is alive and active, walking each step of the way with them.

To Think About
A coincidence is the anonymous presence of God through a small miracle.

Prayer
Lord, help me to recognize you in the miracles of today. Amen.

June

14

"... by your words you will be condemned."
(Matthew 12:37)

Background
This saying underlines the ancient concept of the
spoken word being a dynamic entity. Once spoken,
the word has a life of its own. The speaker of the
word, however, is held responsible for the word that
he or she speaks. If the word becomes an evil force,
the speaker is held responsible. It is the speaker's
responsibility to speak only after great reflection.

Reflection
We are powerless over what happens as a result of
what we say. Once spoken, our words can be open to
misunderstanding and misinterpretation. The words
we speak, or the ones we are purported to have
spoken, can come back to haunt us for many years.
There is much wisdom in G. K. Chesterton's advice:
"I have often regretted having opened my mouth; I
have yet to regret having kept it shut!"

To Think About
The less said, the easiest mended.

Prayer
Lord, grant me a listening heart. Amen.

"Blessed are the peacemakers." (Matthew 5:9)

Background
The word *peacemaker* is normally attributed to one who reconciles quarrels. The Hebrew word *shalom,* means more than the mere absence of trouble; rather, it refers to anything and everything that contributes to a person's highest good. Throughout the Bible, the term shalom connotes an enjoyment of every blessing, of all that is good.

Reflection
A common expression of peacemaking is the hand-shake, which was formerly used to show that one was not armed and intended no harm. It also meant that the person became vulnerable to what the other might do; reaching out an open hand involved taking a risk. If we decide to become peacemakers we not only take a risk, but we must first ensure that we are at peace with ourselves; peace must be personal before it can be communal.

To Think About
Peace cannot be kept by force, it can only be achieved by understanding. (A. Einstein)

Prayer
Lord, make me an instrument of your peace. Amen.

June

16

" . . . and [he] grieved at their hardness of heart."
(Mark 3:5)

Background
Mark is the only Evangelist to mention Jesus' anger,
and the extent of Jesus' opposition to the Pharisees
can be seen in this verse that hints at his anger. The
hardness of the Pharisees' hearts arises from their
interpretation of religion as a ritual. For them, religion means blindly obeying certain rules and
regulations, regardless of the other values that are
at stake.

Reflection
Fanatics in any field can be a danger to both themselves and others. By its very nature, fanaticism
causes us to have tunnel vision. We become so
entrenched in our point of view that we don't even
entertain another's opinion if it does not concur
with ours. All truths must be held in open hands;
they must be constantly examined, without fear, so
they may be better understood.

To Think About
"The truth will set you free." (John 8:32)

Prayer
Lord, may I realize that my sight is limited. Amen.

"Let the children come to me." (Matthew 19:14)

June

17

Background

The disciples realize that Jesus has had a tiring day,
and they want to do their utmost to protect Jesus from
yet further demands on his time and energy in having
to deal with the children. Jesus, however, reminds
his disciples that if they are to receive the message
of the Gospel, they have to have the disposition of
the child. It is the simplicity of children that enables
them to be closer to God than many adults are.

Reflection

When asked why he hasn't progressed beyond teaching seven year olds, an old teacher answers: "By that
time I believe the person is formed, either for better
or for worse." Parents have the privilege of forming
human beings at their most impressionable age.
When we help children form a personal relationship
with Jesus, we give them the greatest gift they'll ever
receive—the gift that will enhance both their living
and their dying.

To Think About

You may give children your love, but not your
thoughts, for they have their own thoughts.
(K. Gibran)

Prayer

Lord, give me childlike faith. Amen.

June

18

"You are the light of the world." *(Matthew 5:14)*

Background

In the context of the Sermon on the Mount, this comparison—along with that of being the "salt of the earth"—introduces the extended passage that is to follow. What ensues will enable Jesus' disciples to learn just how they can become the light of the world and the salt of the earth. It will also teach them the good works by which God will be glorified.

Reflection

George Fox, the founder of the Quakers, used to say that every Quaker should be able to light up the countryside for ten miles around. While Christians do not want to be paraded for their good works, there is no way that goodness can be hidden. Sooner or later it will be seen and, when it is recognized, it becomes self-explanatory. Have you ever heard anyone trying to justify the works of Mother Teresa?

To Think About

People may doubt what I have to say, but they cannot doubt what I do.

Prayer

Lord, may my actions speak louder than my words. Amen.

"Come to me ... and you will find rest for yourselves." (Matthew 11:28-29)

June

19

Background
This saying is peculiar to Matthew's Gospel. Jesus knows that many of his listeners are laboring under the yoke of the Law. By accepting what Jesus has to offer, his listeners receive the promise that they will have the strength they need to carry the day-to-day burdens that come their way.

Reflection
Definitions of happiness can vary from having wealth or possessions, to having everything work out according to plan. Perhaps the greatest definition of happiness is the ability to be content with our lot in life. When the storms of life rage about us, Jesus assures us that he will be there to help us cope. He may not deliver us from hardships, but he will help us endure them and grow by means of them.

To Think About
To have found God is not an end in itself but a beginning. (F. Rosenzweig)

Prayer
Lord, grant me the strength, energy, and vitality to do your will. Amen.

"Ask the master of the harvest to send out laborers for his harvest." (Matthew 9:38)

Background

Jesus and the Pharisees look at the common people but see them from completely different perspectives. For the Pharisees, the common people are mere rubbish to be discarded. For Jesus, the common people are a harvest that is ready for reaping. While the Pharisees want the destruction of sinners, Jesus loves the sinners and eventually gives his life for them.

Reflection

Although many of us Christians desire to give ourselves completely to the Lord and his work, deep inside we feel we can't do that because the circumstances of our lives just aren't "right." If "things" were different, we would be able to give of ourselves fully, the way we want. What we fail to realize is that the harvest is at our feet. God has placed us just where he wants us to work; all he needs is our best effort.

To Think About

I can accomplish more in an hour with God than in a lifetime without him.

Prayer

Open my eyes, Lord, to the vocation I have received. Amen.

"What God has joined together, no human being must separate." (Matthew 19:6)

Background
In the eyes of the Jewish law, a woman is the possession of her father or her husband and, consequently, she has no legal rights. Most Jewish marriages are arranged and the woman often is engaged to be married when she is still a child. She does have the opportunity, however, to refuse the chosen partner when she reaches the age of twelve. Once she is married, the woman can be divorced but she cannot initiate a divorce.

Reflection
Marriage is a commitment that has to be renewed each day. Indeed, there comes a time when the euphoria wears thin and people begin to wonder if perhaps they have made a wrong choice. When we find ourselves within a situation that we cannot get out of, we are often being called to get more into it. If we find no love within a situation, we are called to put some there—and then we will find it.

To Think About
Marriage is our last, best chance to grow up.
(J. Barth)

Prayer
Lord, may I have a forgiving heart and a trusting soul. Amen.

June

22

"Without cost you have received; without cost you are to give." *(Matthew 10:8)*

Background

When Jesus reminds his disciples that they should freely give because they have freely received, he is reiterating a long-established regulation. A rabbi is forbidden to take money for teaching the Law except when he teaches a child, for to teach a child is the parent's task. When those other than the child's parents take on this responsibility, they are entitled to remuneration—but only in this instance.

Reflection

Our world economy works by levying a charge, whether this be for services, time, or lending. Groups who seek to live the Gospel, such as the Amish community, become a cause of wonder because they are exceptional. Before we can allow the gospel to be present in our own little world, we need to set aside the idea of what something is worth and ask ourselves: "What would Jesus do if he were present in this situation?"

To Think About

What would Jesus do?

Prayer

May I recognize you in the beauty all around me. Amen.

"What are you discussing as you walk along?"
(Luke 24:17)

June

23

Background
When the two disciples set out for Emmaus, their whole world is empty. They had hoped for great things from this Jesus of Nazareth but their hopes are shattered with his death and burial. As they walk along the road that day, Jesus begins to explain the reason behind what has happened, and a sense of meaning comes back into the disciples' lives.

Reflection
When we realize that another is within earshot, it may color what we say or how we act. We tend to forget that Jesus said, "I am with you always" (Matthew 28:20). Awareness of Jesus' presence is both an art and a gift. It is a gift that is freely given and it comes through practicing the art of awareness. It is the pearl beyond price that will dispel many a cloud of loneliness on our journey of life.

To Think About
Awareness of the presence of Jesus enables the wheels of life to turn smoothly.

Prayer
Open my eyes, Lord, so that I may recognize you in the ordinary events of my life. Amen.

June

24

"Even all the hairs of your head are counted."
(Matthew 10:30)

Background

Jesus is attempting to show how much God cares for the human person. A sparrow is one of the cheapest items sold in the market. If God knows when this insignificant bird is due to die, surely he is aware of the various details pertaining to the life of every person he himself has created.

Reflection

The reason God doesn't help us when our backs are to the wall is that we don't give him the opportunity. An old Yiddish proverb says that the one who gives us teeth will also give us bread. Trust is often the most fearful lesson we have to learn.

To Think About

Anxiety does not empty tomorrow of its sorrows but only today of its strength.

Prayer

Lord, may I trust in you for little things so that I may learn to trust you for bigger ones. Amen.

*"But the seed sown on rich soil is the one who . . .
bears fruit and yields a hundred or sixty or
thirtyfold."* (Matthew 13:23)

June

25

Background

The parable of the sower can be seen as the early
Church's attempt to classify its various members.
Some seeds—those that fall by the wayside, those
that fall on stony ground, and those that fall among
thorns—are the same as the seed that falls in rich
soil, yet they leave something to be desired. The seed
that falls in rich soil hears, understands, and does
what the gospel commands.

Reflection

A story is told of a teacher who was trying to chide
his student into doing better. "When George
Washington was your age," the teacher said, "he was
head of his class." "Yes, sir," replied the student, "and
when he was your age, he was president of the
United States!" While we may have many things in
common with others, we have some gifts that they
lack and, likewise, they have gifts that we lack.

To Think About

The greatest gift that we can give our world is our
best effort.

Prayer

May I sing my song and thereby embellish the
symphony of life. Amen.

June 26

> "Whoever gives only a cup of cold water to one of these little ones ... he will surely not lose his reward." *(Matthew 10:42)*

Background

The "little ones" that Matthew refers to are the disciples. We are assured that those who extend hospitality to God's messenger will be repaid with the same reward as the messenger. In short, Jesus is telling us that those who help others to be good, in any way, will receive a good person's reward.

Reflection

If we give people fish, they will eat for a day; if we teach them to fish, they will eat for the rest of their lives. If we are thinking a year ahead, we sow seed; if we are thinking ten years ahead, we plant a tree; if we are thinking one hundred years ahead, we educate people. By sowing seed, we will harvest once; by planting a tree, we will harvest tenfold; by educating people, we harvest a hundredfold.

To Think About

Unless a civilization is redeemed spiritually, it cannot endure materially. (W. Wilson)

Prayer

Lord, may I appreciate that whatever I have is meant to be shared with others. Amen.

Then he began to reproach the towns where most of his mighty deeds had been done, since they had not repented. (Matthew 11:20)

Background
The cities of Galilee that have seen and heard Jesus are given privileges that are denied places like Sodom and Gomorrah. The sin the cities of Galilee commit is that they forget the responsibilities of privilege. The greater the privilege, the greater the eventual condemnation if we fail to accept the obligations these privileges bring.

Reflection
We are told that God may provide food but he cannot eat it for us. In a similar way, he will provide us with all of the circumstances necessary for repentance, but he will wait for us to take the first step. Our heavenly Father is like the father of the prodigal son who waited for his son to come to his senses and return home. He didn't follow his son around; he didn't hound his son until he decided to return! Rather, he simply waited.

To Think About
Who errs and mends, to God himself commends.

Prayer
Lord, be merciful to me a sinner. Amen.

June

28

"Although you have hidden these things from the wise and the learned you have revealed them to the childlike." (Matthew 11:25)

Background
This verse forms part of Jesus' prayer of thanksgiving for the success of the mission that has been entrusted to his disciples—the "childlike"—when he sends them out two by two. The "wise and learned" from whom many truths have been hidden are the Jews and especially their leaders, the scribes and the Pharisees, who class themselves as authorities when it comes to the ways of God.

Reflection
Children don't seem to be concerned with the skin color or religion of other children; I have never heard a child refuse to play with another child because of these details. As we grow older, unfortunately, we acquire those prejudices that prevent us from being childlike. The more we live our lives according to gospel values, the more childlike we become. Today let us question what we do and more important, why we do it.

To Think About
Nothing in life is to be feared. It is only to be understood. (M. Curie)

Prayer
Christ is in every event that I encounter this day. Amen.

"My yoke is easy, and my burden light."
(Matthew 11:30)

June

29

Background
The yoke is a wooden implement placed across the neck of an ox that allows the ox to pull the plow. The yoke has to be skillfully made to ensure that it is comfortable for the beast and does not cause chafing on its neck. The Greek word for "easy" is *chrestos,* which means "made to measure." The crosses—the yokes—that Jesus asks us to bear are especially chosen for us.

Reflection
In many cultures women carry heavy loads on their heads. Evidently, the secret to being able to do this lies in perfectly balancing the load. Along those same lines, there is an old proverb: "When Jesus makes a cross for a back, he carefully balances it between the shoulders." When we bring our cross to Jesus, we can rest assured that he will enable us to bear it; left to ourselves we can only despair.

To Think About
When you walk towards the light, the shadow of your burden falls behind you. (K Gibran)

Prayer
Lord, I place at your feet the burdens that weigh me down. Amen.

"See, your disciples are doing what is unlawful to do on the sabbath." (Matthew 12:2)

Background

The disciples are on their way to the synagogue on the Sabbath when they decide to pluck some ears of wheat and rub the grains in their hands to make a simple snack. Yet, the rabbis list the preparation of food as one of the thirty-nine forms of work that is forbidden on the Sabbath. This represents the worst of the Pharisaic interpretation of the Law, and Jesus castigates it.

Reflection

When we focus our attention on rules and regulations, there is always the danger that we will forget the people for whom these rules were made. When we become fanatical about something, an imbalance creeps into our lives, often at the expense of something or someone else. While rules are important, they must always serve the universal law of love.

To Think About

When I plant kindness I reap love.

Prayer

Lord, give me a heart full of love and wonder. Amen.

"Many [people] followed him, and he cured them all." (Matthew 12:15)

July

1

Background

There comes a time in Jesus' ministry when he has to be careful about avoiding a head-on clash with the authorities. He has a mission to accomplish and he has to take care that he allows nothing to curtail its accomplishment. Even though Jesus wants to avoid any unnecessary publicity, the crowds hear of his whereabouts and flock to him.

Reflection

As we learn to follow Jesus, we discover that our priorities and, consequently, our lives change. Many of the worries and tribulations we formerly had are seen from a different perspective and become more manageable. Jesus has the ability to reduce our concerns to their true importance. In this way he brings healing to many situations that we may have felt were impossible.

To Think About

It's the water that gets inside the boat that sinks it, not the oceans about it.

Prayer

Lord, may my journey through life be a journey to a deeper union with you. Amen.

July

2

"Do you want us to go and pull them up?"
(Matthew 13:28)

Background
Darnel among wheat is a familiar occurrence in the lives of Jesus' listeners. Darnel is a weed called tares, and is often called "bastard wheat," because it looks a lot like wheat. In its early stages, in fact, darnel is impossible to distinguish from wheat. Both grow without being distinguishable until it is time for the harvest.

Reflection
It is easier to see the faults of another than it is to see our own; it is also easier to determine what needs to be done about the faults of another than it is to deal with our own faults. We seem to have a natural tendency to "fix" other people. The sad part is that other people are seldom broken! Patience has been defined as the ability to bear or suffer; if we can acquire the virtue of patience, we may find that we develop the ability to reduce the proverbial mountain to a molehill.

To Think About
Let perseverance be perfect so that you may be ... lacking in nothing. (James 1:4)

Prayer
Lord, bless me with patience—in your own good time! Amen.

Hearing what he was doing, a large number of people came to him. (Mark 3:8)

Background
Because of the amount of work that Jesus does, the last thing he wants is a confrontation with synagogue authorities. Consequently, he goes out from the synagogues to the lakeside and the open country. Even there crowds flock to hear him. Fear of being crushed leads him to escape in a boat that gives him safety while still allowing him to preach.

Reflection
Regardless of the field they are in, people usually attract a following when they accomplish something that is considered to be exceptional. As Christians, we are in the business of attracting people to Jesus. The example that we set will speak more clearly than anything we might say.

To Think About
It is better to keep quiet and be, than to make fluent professions and not be. (Saint Ignatius of Antioch)

Prayer
May my life not contradict what I say. Amen.

His mother and his brothers appeared outside, wishing to speak with him. (Matthew 12:46)

Background
Some scholars conjecture that the term "his brothers" may refer to the children of Joseph by a former marriage. Others believe that they are the children of Mary's sister, the wife of Cleophas. The first interpretation, however, is the most natural. There is also the custom of referring to kinsmen as brothers. There are no references in the New Testament or in other sources that clearly indicate Mary had other children.

Reflection
Many people do not find Jesus within a church setting and yet they wish to speak with him. It may be, then, that we are the only contact these people will have with Jesus. Yet, although we might speak eloquently and with best intentions of how good Jesus is, we may succeed in alienating these people even further. It is often our silent witness that will speak most clearly, even if it appears to fall on deaf ears.

To Think About
Silent witness is one of the hardest arguments to refute.

Prayer
May others come to know you through their contact with me. Amen.

"And as he sowed, some seed fell on the path, and the birds came and ate it up." (Matthew 13:4)

July
5

Background
In Palestine at the time of Jesus, fields are long narrow strips of land and the dividing ground between them are common paths that become hardened as people walk on them. The most common way of sowing seed is for the farmer to walk up and down the field scattering the seed by hand. It is easy to see how some seed could fall on the pathways.

Reflection
Because of their past or present situations, some people find themselves unable to fulfill their full potential, feeling as if their lives are wasted—like the seed lying by the side of the path. However, this is the seed that becomes food for the birds; God uses it to give life in a way that we could never have expected. If we trust God, he will use us in ways we never thought possible.

To Think About
If I want to see God's sense of humor, I tell him my plans.

Prayer
Lord, light my path so that I may see. Amen.

July

6

"Gross is the heart of this people." (Matthew 13:15)

Background

Jesus is always concerned with the intentions that motivate a person. He denounces the Pharisees, for example, even when they are praying, because their intention is not to praise God but to seek their own glorification. Here again, Jesus indicts those who are so prejudiced against him that they have closed their hearts off from the possibility of hearing the truth.

Reflection

If a couple is to retain the vitality and life-giving nature of their marriage, they have to work on their relationship. Each day the couple needs to begin as if they had just received the sacrament. One of the greatest dangers is that the couple will come to take each other for granted. The same thing is true in living the Christian life. We must live each day as if we had just been converted. Each day is a new beginning with Jesus—a new day to live for Jesus.

To Think About

Each venture is a new beginning. (T. S. Eliot)

Prayer

Give me a new and steadfast heart with which to serve you and others this day. Amen.

"The evil one comes and steals away what was sown in his heart." (Matthew 13:19)

July
7

Background
The effect God's word has on people is determined by the disposition of their hearts. Quite often, a person will not understand because there is no love in his or her heart. We are told that a lack of love is what opens the door of the soul to the evil one, that the only thing more harmful than a closed mind is a closed heart.

Reflection
When Jesus lists the things that prevent the seed from yielding as much fruit as it could, he mentions tribulations, persecution, anxieties, and the lure of riches. Quite often, the best way to counteract a weakness is to cultivate the opposite strength. Love alone will enable us to hear and respond to what Jesus is asking of us. Today is a new beginning and today we need a new commitment to loving.

To Think About
The shadows are merely a reflection of my fears.

Prayer
Lord, open the doors you would have me open and close the doors you would have me close. Amen.

July

8

"If you pull up the weeds you might uproot the wheat along with them." (Matthew 13:29)

Background

Because the darnel looks so similar to the wheat while it is growing, it is impossible to differentiate between the two. However, when it has grown, its difference can be easily spotted. By then, of course, its roots have become so intertwined with the roots of the wheat that it is impossible to pull one without pulling the other.

Reflection

As Scripture tells us, there is a season for everything under heaven (see Ecclesiastes 3:1). There is a time when the faults and shortcomings of others have to be confronted, and a time when we have to turn the proverbial "blind eye." If we do not carefully pick our time and place for confronting, we risk doing more harm than good. True wisdom lies in knowing when and how to confront in love.

To Think About

A good run can often be better than a bad stand. (Irish proverb)

Prayer

Lord, give me the grace to change the things I can change, the strength to endure the things I cannot change, and the wisdom to know the difference. Amen.

"The kingdom of heaven is like a treasure buried in a field." (Matthew 13:44)

July
9

Background

In Jesus' time there is always the danger of invasion by a foreign power. If this ever became imminent, a householder would bury his treasure in the hope of finding it safe and secure when he returned. Jesus does not pass judgment on the ethics of the finder, but points to his conduct as an example of the zeal with which the believer should pursue the kingdom of God.

Reflection

Within the field of life, there are many treasures, such as health, reputation, possessions, etc. For Christians, following Jesus is central to all of these. It is this that gives true value and worth to everything and everyone. When Jesus holds the prime place in our lives, we are no longer possessed by our possessions or driven by fruitless ambitions; rather, all things fall into proper perspective.

To Think About

What makes me rich is not what I have but what I value.

Prayer

Lord, you are my treasure. Amen.

"It is the smallest of all the seeds, yet when full-grown it is the largest of plants." *(Matthew 13:32)*

Background
While being relatively small, the mustard seed is by no means the smallest of seeds. Neither is the mustard tree the "largest of plants" when it is full grown; in fact, it would be more accurate to call it a shrub. The point that Jesus is making is the contrast that exists between the word of God as a small seed and the large effects it can have on human life.

Reflection
Human seed ranks among the smallest of seeds, yet it is the most important. It is the vehicle by which the kingdom of God on earth will be transmitted. When we reflect on the potential of the human seed, given the proper circumstances, the mind boggles! Any human has the potential to surpass our wildest dreams, either for good or for bad. Let us reverence each child for what he or she is and for what he or she is destined to become.

To Think About
You have made them [humans] little less than a god. (Psalm 8:6)

Prayer
May I see your glory reflected in every person who crosses my path this day. Amen.

"Whoever has ears ought to hear." (Matthew 13:43)

July
11

Background
The process of salvation begins in the heart by receiving the word of God. Rejection of this testimony, on the other hand, hardens the heart. Hardness of heart shows itself in many ways, especially by our unwillingness to listen. Jesus himself upbraids the Pharisees because they have closed their minds to what he says to them and, consequently, they reject the possibility of "be[ing] converted and be[ing] forgiven" (Mark 4:12).

Reflection
Listening is an art that is practiced with the heart. To hear another correctly we must first open our hearts to the speaker. Only in that way can we hear what he or she is truly trying to say. Although God often speaks to us through another, we often reject his message because we are unable to accept the speaker. Today, let us reverence those who speak to us so that we may truly hear what they are saying.

To Think About
It is the privilege of wisdom to listen.
(O. Wendell Holmes)

Prayer
Speak, Lord, your servant is listening. Amen.

July

12

"When he finds a pearl of great price, he goes and sells all that he has and buys it."
(Matthew 13:46)

Background

In this parable Jesus is showing us the supreme value of the kingdom of heaven and the attitude people need if they are to attain it. It is rather interesting to note that finding the pearl is the result of a lengthy search, whereas finding the treasure (see Matthew 13:44) is something rather happenstance—it just happens. In this distinction we see that detachment and generosity are indispensable for obtaining the kingdom.

Reflection

It can often take a near tragedy to bring us to our senses and make us appreciate what we take for granted. Bringing about the kingdom of heaven is the most important thing to a Christian. Today, it might prove helpful if we pause from time to time to ask ourselves if what we are doing is, in fact, helping to create heaven on earth. If not, it is not worth doing.

To Think About

Fellowship is heaven and lack of fellowship is hell.
(W. Morris)

Prayer

Lord, guide me today in what you would have me do. Amen.

"Lord, if you had been here, my brother would not have died." (John 11:21)

July

13

Background

The Martha who speaks these words is true to her character. She is a person of action who doesn't allow the proverbial grass to grow under her feet. As soon as Jesus arrives, for example, she reproaches him for delaying. No sooner are these words spoken, however, than she breaks forth into a beautiful act of faith in Jesus' special relationship to the Father: "Even now I know that whatever you ask of God, God will give you" (John 11:22).

Reflection

There is a unique finality about death. On a human level, death confronts us with an insurmountable brick wall. For one who believes in what Jesus promises, however, death is just a stepping stone to another, more lasting life. When Jesus is present within a situation—even one that involves death— there is hope and, therefore, there is life. Jesus is the light who alone can dispel the darkness of any cross.

To Think About

When a shadow crosses my life it may be because Jesus is passing by.

Prayer

The Lord is my shepherd, there is nothing I shall want. Amen.

July

14

"Is he not the carpenter's son?"
(Matthew 13:55)

Background

The Nazarenes' surprise, as expressed in this brief question, is to some extent due to the difficulty they have in recognizing anything exceptional and supernatural in one with whom they have been on familiar terms. Being unaware of the mystery of Jesus' conception, they are jealous of the wisdom he displays.

Reflection

The world judges people according to what they produce or what they own, rather than by who they are. As a result, we tend to categorize others into the "successful" and the "also ran," into the "acceptable" and the "unacceptable." As Christians, we must realize that each individual is a child who is infinitely loved by the Father. Today, we are called to move from categorizing to realizing.

To Think About

Every time I paint a portrait, I lose a friend.
(J. Singer Sargent)

Prayer

Lord, may the least of your people be treated with dignity and respect. Amen.

For John had said to him, "It is not lawful for you to have her." (Matthew 14:4)

July
15

Background
Herod Antipas has a brother in Rome whom the gospel writers called Herod Philip. He is quite wealthy but does not have a kingdom of his own. He is married and, on a visit to Rome, Herod Antipas seduces his wife, Herodias. As a result, Herod Antipas marries Herodias, thereby necessitating the putting aside of his own wife, the daughter of the king of the Nabatean Arabs.

Reflection
For many, the popular term "dumbing down" has come to mean making things simpler. There is the danger, however, that "dumbing down" can imply a lowering of standards. Our times need people who will stand up for what is right, against all odds, just because it is the right thing to do. Being on the side of truth and lawfulness may not make us the most popular person on the block, but it will assure us of a good night's sleep.

To Think About
Knowledge without integrity is dangerous and dreadful. (S. Johnson)

Prayer
Lord, let your light shine within me that I may radiate your love to all. Amen.

July

16

> *"Five loaves and two fish are all we have here."*
> *Then he said, "Bring them here to me."*
> *(Matthew 14:17-18)*

Background

Five loaves and two fish are hardly enough to feed Jesus and the apostles. Some scholars interpret this miracle as individuals sharing what they had and, from the collected amount, there was more than enough to feed everyone. If this is what happened, the real miracle is not the multiplication of the loaves and fish but the changing of people from being selfish to being selfless.

Reflection

When confronted with problems, all too often we become aware of our limitations, i.e., our mere five loaves and two fish. It is then, however, that Jesus is at his most powerful as he tells us: "Bring them here to me." However small our talents may appear, Jesus can work miracles with them. If he can feed over five thousand people with five loaves and a few fish, what can he do with our lives if they are given to him?

To Think About

God wants nothing of us but our cooperation.

Prayer

Lord, take my small gifts and make them great for your sake. Amen.

"O you of little faith, why did you doubt?"
(Matthew 14:31)

Background

As we read and reflect on the Gospels, we find that
Peter tends to allow his heart to rule his head.
Because he so often acts on impulse, he comes to
grief. Peter, however, never fully fails because he
always reaches out for Jesus when he knows that a
situation is hopeless. He falls, time and again, but he
always gets up and begins again.

Reflection

An old Greek proverb states that "the wise are prone
to doubt." As a person searches for truth, doubts will
arise time and again. Doubt is an essential ingredi-
ent in the process of growth, and it is the crucible in
which all of our truths are sifted. If we are prepared
to rest with honest doubt, we will eventually come to
a certitude that nothing and nobody will be able to
undermine.

To Think About

If I could not doubt, I should not believe.
(H. D. Thoreau)

Prayer

Lord, help thou my unbelief. Amen.

July

18

"If a blind person leads a blind person, both will fall into a pit." (Matthew 15:14)

Background

Jesus has just told the Pharisees that their observance of the laws dealing with food is meaningless because it lacks the proper motivation. By placing such an emphasis on the external observance of such laws, the Pharisees are like blind guides who do not know what the way to God really looks like. Those who follow the Pharisees can only expect to stray off the road and fall into a pit or a ditch.

Reflection

In spite of what we may think, all of us exert influence on others—for good or bad. Without realizing it, people often ape our conduct. As Christians, it is our privilege to attract others to Jesus. This presupposes, of course, that our hearts are set on him. If we are living for him, he will use us to draw others to himself. If we lead, we can rest assured that others will follow.

To Think About

"Come after me, and I will make you fishers of men." (Matthew 4:19)

Prayer

Lead me, Lord, and I will follow. Amen.

But he did not say a word in answer to her.
(Matthew 15:23)

July

19

Background
Jesus, finished with a busy day of ministering, is headed for a few hours of quiet when he finds himself confronted by a Canaanite woman—Canaanites being the sworn enemies of the Jews. Yet, here he is confronted with a Gentile woman who pleads on behalf of her child.

Reflection
Listening to God has been compared to listening to a radio. To hear what is being transmitted, we must first make sure the radio is turned on. In the same way, we must be sure that we are switched on to God through our desire for him. Second, we must be sure that we have our radio tuned to the right wavelength. In our spiritual lives, we are on the right wavelength when we do what God wants of us. Third, the volume on our radio must be such that we can hear what is being broadcast. In the same way we must adjust the volume of our lives—often through silence—if we are to hear what God has to say.

To Think About
People talking without speaking, people hearing without listening . . . . (P. Simon)

Prayer
Lord, you have the words of everlasting life. Amen.

July

20

"Whatever you loose on earth shall be loosed in heaven." *(Matthew 16:19)*

Background

Jesus speaks these words to Peter, the person he chooses to be the leader of the early Church. Jesus implies that Peter will be the one responsible for making decisions that will direct the life and destiny of the newborn Church. When we read the Acts of the Apostles we find that this is precisely what Peter does.

Reflection

How often we have heard the words of Alexander Pope: "To err is human, to forgive divine." Until we decide to forgive, those who have wronged us are not free to move on with their lives, and we remain emotionally and spiritually imprisoned. Ironically, it is only when we have granted forgiveness that we ourselves are free to approach God and ask for our own forgiveness.

To Think About

He who forgives ends the quarrel. (African proverb)

Prayer

Lord, as for those who have wronged me, give me a forgiving heart and a poor memory. Amen.

But Jesus came and touched them. (Matthew 17:7)

July
21

Background
This passage comes at the end of Jesus' transfiguration. A short time before this, Jesus tells his disciples that he is destined to suffer and die. As a result, the disciples' faith in Jesus is shattered as they begin to realize that he is not going to be the victorious conqueror they had hoped he would be. This experience strengthens the disciples for the dark days that lie ahead.

Reflection
Others can touch us in many ways. When we are touched with reverence—physically, emotionally, or spiritually—we are changed, and this change can often have a lasting effect. By the same token, each time we interact with others, whether it is through the spoken word or a simple gesture, we touch them—and they are better or worse for having encountered us.

To Think About
Move along these shades in gentleness of heart; with gentle hand touch—for there is a spirit in the woods. (W. Wordsworth)

Prayer
Lord, may the inner beauty of your creation evoke a profound reverence in me. Amen.

July

22

"*Bring him here to me.*" (Matthew 17:17)

Background
No sooner does Jesus and the three disciples come
down from the mountain of the transfiguration than
they are confronted with human suffering in the
form a man who brings his epileptic son to be
healed. The disciples fail to help the boy but the
father knows that Jesus can succeed. Indeed, Jesus
gives the command: "Bring him here to me."

Reflection
When we love others, we want to "give them the
world," although we know this is beyond our capa-
bility. Instead, we give those we love to Jesus, who
alone can bless them with the abundance we cannot
offer. Praying for others is one of the most powerful
ways of expressing our love for them—and we can
express our love in this way at any time.

To Think About
It is possible to give without loving, but it is impossible to love without wanting to give.

Prayer
Lord, I give to you all of my loved ones so that you
may bless them as you wish. Amen.

"It is I; do not be afraid." (Matthew 14:27)

Background
Storms occur frequently on Lake Gennesaret, often creating huge waves that are dangerous for small fishing boats. While Jesus is praying on the hillside, he notices the disciples battling one of these storms, and he comes to their aid. Initially the disciples are frightened when they see him, but Jesus tells them not to be afraid for he is now with them.

Reflection
We have all experienced fear: fear at the prospect of meeting someone; fear of something from our past being discovered; fear of a pending event. Fear can be real or imaginary, and it can express itself in many forms. Quite often lack of love lies at the root of fear. Whatever form our fear takes, Jesus says: "You are not alone; I'm already there."

To Think About
I need not be afraid of the future because Jesus is already there.

Prayer
Lord, shine the light of your love within me that it may cast out the darkness of fear. Amen.

July
24

"Go to the sea, drop in a hook, and take the first fish that comes up...." (Matthew 17:27)

Background
Because of the cost involved in running the Temple, a tax is levied on every male Jew over the age of twenty years. The tax is equivalent to two days' pay. After the fall of Jerusalem in 70 A.D., however, the tax is collected by the Roman emperor for the upkeep of the temple of Jupiter Capitolinus in Rome. For the Jews, this is a bitter pill to swallow, something they detest.

Reflection
We cannot expect God to do for us what we can do for ourselves. Our job is a blessing and, while we may not have the job of our dreams, we should cherish the situation as an opportunity.

To Think About
Lord you have a special task for me that only I can perform.

Prayer
Lord, thank you for calling me worthy to work for you. Amen.

"Whoever loves his life loses it." (John 12:25)

Background
This passage echoes Paul's comment about Christ humbling himself and becoming obedient unto death—even death on a cross—and God the Father exalting him above all created things. For people to be supernaturally effective, they have to die to their own needs. Individual comfort must always be secondary to the call of Christ.

Reflection
It has been said that life is similar to a hand of cards: It isn't the cards you are dealt that matters but the way you play them. While we have a duty to do everything within our power to remain healthy, a life centered on self is a life imprisoned within the confines of selfishness. By reaching out to others, we enlarge the horizons of our world. This, ultimately, is what gives lasting value to life.

To Think About
The love of our neighbor is the only door out of the dungeon of self. (G. McDonald)

Prayer
Lord, help me to focus on others and not on myself. Amen.

July

26

"If two of you agree on earth about anything for which they are to pray, it shall be granted to them by my heavenly Father." (Matthew 18:19)

Background

This verse appears to reflect a more developed concept of the Church. As those who have ever prayed for anything know, we are not always granted that which we ask for, no more than children are given everything they ask for from their loving parents. While we may not always be given what we want, we are always given what we need, especially when our prayer is united with that of our brothers and sisters.

Reflection

If one person stands outside a meeting hall and protests, that person will probably be considered an eccentric. If that person joins one million other people in protest, collectively they will be heard. Just as we can never underestimate the power of public opinion, we can never underestimate the power of unity. It is unity that authenticates all of our prayer and it is unity that lies at the center of our Christian lives, i.e., the Eucharist.

To Think About

Strength united is greater. (Latin proverb)

Prayer

Lord, give me a loving heart so that I may join with my brothers and sisters in discovering the true meaning of community. Amen.

"Everything is possible to one who has faith."
(Mark 9:23)

July
27

Background
As happens many times in the Gospels, Jesus requires faith before he can work a miracle. When the man's faith is strengthened, he becomes all-powerful because he no longer relies on his own resources, but on Jesus Christ. It is as if, through faith, we become partakers in God's omnipotence, and everything becomes possible to us.

Reflection
Thomas Edison patented in excess of one thousand inventions. In fact, he founded a factory—Menlo Park—specifically for making inventions. There he promised to produce a minor invention every ten days and a major one every six months. Edison was successful because he believed that inventions were waiting to be made. If we believe that with God we are invincible, nothing can overpower us.

To Think About
If God is for me who can be against me?

Prayer
Lord, together we can do great things. Amen.

July

28

"If anyone wishes to be first, he shall be the last of all and the servant of all." (Mark 9:35)

Background
Jesus, hearing the argument about who will be most important among the disciples, uses the situation to teach about the proper use of authority in the Church. True power does not consist of lording it over others but of serving others. Service is both the hallmark and greatest exercise of authority.

Reflection
Saint Francis of Assisi is reputed to have said that one would have to stand on one's head in order to see things from God's perspective. So it is with the values that Jesus preaches, for these values are often directly opposed to the values of our world. Our world says: "To be great, accumulate wealth and gain power." Jesus says: "Become like little children." Which way will we go?

To Think About
Many who choose to serve God do so by becoming his advisors!

Prayer
Lord, may I appreciate that love is the measure of service. Amen.

"For whoever is not against us is for us."
(Mark 9:40)

July
29

Background

There is always the danger that we will consider our interpretation of a situation to be the only one, to the exclusion of all others. The early disciples have to learn to appreciate that there are as many paths to God as there are people. Because God is Father of all humankind, there are no favorites, and exclusivity cannot have a part in the apostolate.

Reflection

In an effort to explain how people who have never heard of Jesus Christ can live according to the values that Jesus preached, the theologian Karl Rahner spoke of the "anonymous Christian." Today there are many people who have never darkened chapel or church yet who would put us to shame when it comes to loving their neighbor. Until we appreciate that Jesus is at work in the most unexpected of people, we will fail to experience the wonders he wants to shower on us.

To Think About

When God measures my greatness, he measures my heart, not my head.

Prayer

Lord, open my eyes to your presence in those about me. Amen.

July

30

"Salt is good, but if salt becomes insipid, with what will you restore its flavor?" (Mark 9:50)

Background
Salt has two main functions: to preserve food from going bad and to add flavor to food. There was the ancient belief that nothing was purer than salt because it came from the two purest things in the universe: the sun and the sea. Followers of Jesus have a similar purpose. They have to prevent society from its human tendency to become corrupt, and society must be the better for their presence.

Reflection
To be human is to be prone to failure. The only thing we can claim as our own is sin. Yet, the beauty of the Christian calling is that despite sin, we are given a second chance. This is the very purpose of Jesus' coming. He himself assures us: "I came not to call the righteous but the sinner to repent." It is never too late to change our lives; it is never too late to make a new beginning.

To Think About
Honest people become honest by the choices they make.

Prayer
Lord, help me to see your will for me. Amen.

"Now is the Son of Man glorified, and God is glorified in him." (John 13:31)

Background
The Evangelist John considers Christ's death to be the beginning of his glorification. It is by means of his crucifixion that Jesus takes the first step along the path of his ascension to his Father. By freely accepting death as a supreme act of obedience to the will of God, Jesus performs the greatest sacrifice anyone can offer for the glorification of God.

Reflection
After his conversion, Saint Ignatius of Loyola, the founder of the Society of Jesus, was motivated by the simple dictum *Ad maiorem Dei gloriam:* "To the greater glory of God." His fellow Jesuits have made this their guiding rule of life. Is it any wonder that we cannot even begin to estimate the enormous contribution that the Jesuits, and other religious orders, have made to the work of the Church.

To Think About
If I seek to glorify God by my own efforts, the results will be found wanting.

Prayer
Glory be to the Father, the Son, and the Holy Spirit. Amen.

July
31

"The Mighty One has done great things for me."
(Luke 1:49)

Background

The Magnificat overflows with Old Testament principles. It is similar to the song of Hannah, for example, found in 1 Samuel 2:1-10, where Hannah sings God's praises for the great things he has done for her. Mary's Magnificat has become one of the most popular and frequently used hymns of the Church.

Reflection

Each woman is born with thousands of eggs that are capable of being fertilized later in life. Of all these eggs, God determines that a particular one will result in a unique human being, unlike any other human being in all eternity. God renews that act of creation each morning as he blesses each of us with the gift of another day, a new beginning, a day unlike any other in all eternity. Not until we begin to count our blessings will we be able to appreciate how great are the things that the Mighty One has done for us.

To Think About

Many a blessing is so well wrapped that I fail to recognize it at first sight.

Prayer

Lord, thank you for showering me with your love. Amen.

"If you wish to enter into life, keep the commandments." (Matthew 19:17)

August

2

Background
It is rather interesting that when Jesus tells the young man to keep the commandments, he doesn't recite them in the order in which they are found in the Decalogue, which would make it look like he was placing greater value on some over others. The five that Jesus does cite, however, are ones taken from the second part of the Decalogue, the part that deals with our duty to humankind rather than our duty to God.

Reflection
The clarity of the Gospels has the ability to rivet us where we are at any moment. Jesus tells us that he has come to offer life, life in abundance. However, he comes to offer it, not impose it. In his direct but simple way, he tells us that obedience to the commandments is the gateway to this life. If we live our lives according to its dictates, we will experience what he offers. If not, we must accept the consequences.

To Think About
The devil does not fear austerity but holy obedience. (Saint Francis de Sales)

Prayer
Lord, you will never let go of me; may I never let go of you. Amen.

August

3

"For he had many possessions." (Matthew 19:22)

Background

The story of the rich young man is the story of one of life's greatest tragedies. Because this young man has great possessions—rather, they have him—he makes the great refusal. By drawing on the comparison of the camel trying to negotiate the narrow gate, called a needle, Jesus tries to show that it is impossible for people who put their heart on worldly things to have a part in the kingdom of God.

Reflection

Wealth is relative. Being poor in a middle-class country might mean being a millionaire in a Third World country. It's not so much what we have that is important but rather, what has us! Like all gifts, wealth is given to us to be used. What we give away to others will go before us beyond the grave; what we hold on to, will die with us.

To Think About

God calls me to give my time, talent, and treasure to the least of his people.

Prayer

Lord, teach me to be generous, to give without counting the cost! Amen.

"These last ones worked only one hour, and you have made them equal to us, who bore the day's burden and the heat." (Matthew 20:12)

August
4

Background

This parable gives a small insight into the appalling condition of casual labor in the Hellenistic-Roman world. Because the grape crop doesn't ripen until late September, there is always the fear that the rains, which come shortly afterwards, will destroy the crop. As a result, immediate harvesting is essential. Hence the need to hire laborers—even at the eleventh hour.

Reflection

God's ways are certainly not our ways. From a human standpoint, God often appears to deal with us in an unfair way. How often we hear the cry: "Why me?" and the only response appears to be: "Why not you?" When we learn to trust God, we come to appreciate that he wants only what is best for us, even though at the time it may not appear that way. As we learn to trust, we grow to appreciate the fact that all will be well.

To Think About

Life is a process of learning to trust—and it is a difficult apprenticeship.

Prayer

Lord, teach me to trust in you. Amen.

August

5

" ... everything is ready; come to the feast."
(Matthew 22:4)

Background

When an invitation to a feast, such as a wedding
banquet, is issued, it is done in two stages. First, a
servant is sent to the invited guests well in advance
of the occasion to alert them of the date of the feast.
As that date draws near, when everything is ready
and specific plans have been made, servants are sent
out again with the final summons.

Reflection

Deep in our subconscious minds we often think: "I
must get around to doing something about ..." or
words to that effect. Little do we appreciate that
"now" is the time when a grace or strength is given
for some good work. Unless we learn to act on what
God is prompting us to do, we run the risk of losing
the opportunity of a lifetime—because the moment
will never return.

To Think About

Yesterday is a memory, tomorrow is a promise, today
is all I have.

Prayer

Lord, may I realize that now is the acceptable time.
Amen.

"You shall love the Lord, your God, with all your heart." (Matthew 22:37)

August

6

Background
This text is taken from Deuteronomy 6:5 and forms the central core of the Jewish faith. Every Jewish service, to this day, opens with the recitation of this verse, and every Jewish child is expected to commit it to memory. It simply means that the love of God must be the driving force that motivates all our thoughts and actions.

Reflection
When we love another, our love finds expression through the little things we do for that person. Our love for God is no different. As we grow deeper and deeper in love with him, we will find ourselves asking: "What would Jesus want of me if he were here right now?" Initially, we may have to make an effort to consciously ask this question. Eventually, however, it will become a habit.

To Think About
God forces no one, for love cannot compel.
(H. Denk)

Prayer
Lord, may my life be a reflection of your love. Amen.

August

7

"Whoever does not accept the kingdom of God like a child will not enter it." (Mark 10:15)

Background

This verse sheds light on the qualities that are necessary if we are to enter and live within the kingdom of God. By their very nature, children demonstrate qualities such as obedience, trust, openness, and a lack of prejudice. All these qualities are essential to accepting and living the gospel message.

Reflection

Children can teach us a lot. Have you ever noticed how adults, when given a gift, will often tell the donor, "Oh, you should not have bothered." How many of us, however, have ever heard a child utter a comment like this. Children accept all that is given without a word, often adding: "Is this all?" Jesus comes to share with us the life of the kingdom. When will we have the courage to accept what he wants to give unconditionally?

To Think About

The secret of contentment is realizing that life is a gift, freely given.

Prayer

Lord, thank you for the many gifts you have given me. Amen.

"Go, therefore, and make disciples of all nations."
(Matthew 28:19)

August

8

Background
This verse comes toward the end of Matthew's Gospel and gives us an insight into the early Church's understanding of its mission. For quite some time, the apostolic Church understood its mission to involve a ministry to only the Jews. Here Jesus says that this restriction no longer exists; the mission is understood to involve all nations.

Reflection
The greatest river begins as a mere trickling of water. As it journeys from its source, it gathers strength and becomes a stream. Eventually, it becomes a raging torrent and finally a mighty river, gaining in size and strength until it reaches the ocean. When we work for Jesus we may be able to do only small things for him, but he will use our small efforts in mighty ways.

To Think About
Not every converted person has converting power.

Prayer
Lord, use even my smallest efforts to build your mighty kingdom. Amen.

August

9

"Go, sell what you have, and give to [the] poor and you will have treasure in heaven; then come, follow me." (Mark 10:21)

Background

Absolute renunciation as a condition for following Jesus applies to more than mere wealth. In the story of the rich young man, it would appear that the man's wealth is mentioned only incidentally, but the symbolism is significant. The only way to eternal life is to follow Jesus and to renounce absolutely anything that may come between oneself and him.

Reflection

A story is told of two islanders who came to the mainland and got drunk. In the dark of night, they went to their boat, clambered aboard, and began to row. As the first light of dawn began to brighten the sky, they wondered why they had made no progress. Then they realized that they hadn't loosened the mooring. Many are incapable of entering the kingdom of heaven because they fail to throw off earthly shackles, to loosen the moorings that chain them to earthly riches.

To Think About

Anything I hold in my hands may be lost; anything I place in God's hands can never be lost.

Prayer

Lord, may I count everything as loss compared to following you. Amen.

The disciples then went off, entered the city, and found it just as he had told them. (Mark 14:16)

Background

Jesus does not leave things until the last moment, and he seems to leave nothing to chance. His disciples, wanting to know where they are going to eat the Passover, are told that they will see a man carrying an earthen pitcher of water. Now this is routinely a woman's duty, and so a man with a water pot on his shoulder will be conspicuous. Once contact is made with this man, everything else will follow.

Reflection

It has been said that faith is not so much a matter of believing without proof as trusting without reservation. When we do anything for Jesus, he will always provide us with the means, if only we are prepared to trust him. In asking us to be his witnesses in the world, he has given us the strength we need; he has given us no less a gift than his own body and blood—a gift that can be ours each day that we live.

To Think About

I have the strength for everything through him who empowers me. (Philippians 4:13)

Prayer

Lord, take me and transform me into a living image of your body and blood. Amen.

August
10

August 11

"The stone which the builders rejected has become the cornerstone." (Mark 12:10)

Background

Israel's leaders reject Jesus as the Messiah, and yet he becomes the capstone of God's new people. Clearly the parable is a renunciation of Israel's religious leaders and what they stand for. He himself will be selected over them, even though they are convinced that they are the divinely chosen ones.

Reflection

A woman takes her young son to a concert given by the famous pianist, Paderewski. As they wait for the performance to begin, the boy becomes impatient and wanders onto the stage, where he begins to play "Bah Bah Black Sheep" on the piano. When the pianist realizes what's happening, he comes on stage, stands behind the boy, and whispers "Don't stop," as he begins to add a bass part and an obbligato. When they finish, they receive a standing ovation. When God chooses us, he makes something beautiful of our efforts.

To Think About

God is more concerned with my availability than with my ability.

Prayer

Thank you, O Lord, for transforming my weakness into something beautiful. Amen.

"You shall love your neighbor as yourself."
(Matthew 22:39)

August
12

Background
Those who wish to love must be prepared to forget themselves. The command to love is the most important commandment because in obeying it, we attain perfection. Because of its prime importance, this commandment is placed at the center of the gospel challenge, and it summarizes our duty to both God and humankind.

Reflection
Neighbors noticed that the house where the elderly bachelor lived was unoccupied and that the lawn had become overgrown. They made inquiries and found that the occupant had taken a trip abroad and had been involved in an accident. Together, as neighbors, they decided to assume the upkeep of the property. Not only was the property kept in good condition, but the work brought the neighborhood closer together as a community. As we reach out in love to the neighbor, we cannot help loving ourselves.

To Think About
The supreme reality of our time is our indivisibility as children of God. (J. K. Kennedy)

Prayer
Let me recognize you in every face I see. Amen.

August

13

... and immediately blood and water flowed out.
(John 19:34)

Background

The water that flows from the wound made in Jesus' side at the crucifixion is probably an accumulation of liquid in the lungs due to his intense sufferings. As with many of John's references, this one is laden with meaning. Christian tradition, dating mainly from the time of Saint Augustine, sees the sacraments and the Church itself flowing from Jesus' open side.

Reflection

To emphasize our love for another, we often say: "I would give my life for that person"—and this is precisely what Jesus does. The only way in which we can ever hope to repay love is with love. We can show our love for Jesus in the ways we treat those about us, for Jesus says that whatever we do to one of the least, we do it to him.

To Think About

Loving means knowing how to do ordinary things with tenderness. (Jean Vanier)

Prayer

Lord, help me to know that there is no limit to your love for me. Amen.

A poor woman also came and put in two small coins worth a few cents ... all she had.
(Mark 12:42, 44)

Background
In the Court of the Women, within the Temple at Jerusalem, there are thirteen collection boxes called Trumpets, so called because of their shape. Each box is for a special purpose. The coins that the woman flings are called lepton, which literally means "a thin one." It is the smallest of all coins and is worth one-fortieth of one pence.

Reflection
When a thimble and a bucket are filled to capacity, the bucket holds a greater volume of water than the thimble. However, both are full and incapable of holding one drop more. When we give our all to God, it may appear that others have given far more than we have. But ours is not to judge; at best we can only hope that God, who sees the desire of our hearts, will use us in his service.

To Think About
It's not the gift but what it signifies that counts.

Prayer
Lord, may your wish be mine. Amen.

"Most blessed are you among women, and blessed is the fruit of your womb." *(Luke 1:42)*

Background

Elizabeth's greeting is a form of lyrical song about the blessedness of Mary. In the Old Testament (see Genesis 24:60; 1 Samuel 2:20) we find that one blesses another by expressing good wishes or offering prayers to God for the person's welfare. Mary realizes that she is truly blessed but she never loses sight of the source of her blessing: "The Almighty has done great things to me!" (see Luke 1:49).

Reflection

Young Ricky had many gifts but acting wasn't one of them. When the day came for assigning parts in the school play, Ricky's mother felt he would be disappointed. When she went to pick him up after school, however, he ran to meet her, wild with excitement. "Mom, they have picked me to clap and cheer!"
God has a plan that, like Mary and Ricky, only I can fulfill!

To Think About

An outstanding life is the sum of excellent moments.

Prayer

Lord, may I appreciate the dignity of my calling. Amen.

When his relatives heard of this they set out to seize him, for they said, "He is out of his mind."
(Mark 3:21)

August
16

Background
Some of Jesus' close relations understand neither his commitment to his Father nor the way in which this commitment has to be lived out. They regard Jesus' commitment to his mission as excessive. The only explanation they can come up with is that Jesus is out of his mind. Throughout the course of history, many saints have been considered mad merely because of the extent of their commitment to God.

Reflection
Parents sometimes think they know what is best for their children, when actually they are simply trying to live out their own unfulfilled dreams and ambitions through their kids. While it's only natural that they want to protect their young, parents must never forget that children are only on loan to them. God has a plan for these children, and parents must pray that their children discover what that plan is—because it holds the key to their children's happiness.

To Think About
Since God's knows best, why not ask his advice rather than giving advice to him.

Prayer
Let nothing prevent me from doing the right thing, Lord. Amen.

August
17

"Blessed are the peacemakers." (Matthew 5:9)

Background
The beatitudes are not part of a single sermon; rather, they are the collection of the salient points Jesus makes during his public ministry. In listening to Jesus as he proclaims "blessed are," we share the kernel of what Jesus wishes to communicate to his disciples. It is important to remember that those who try to live by the beatitudes are not promised happiness merely in the next life; rather, they are promised happiness in this life as well.

Reflection
Peace is what happens when my relationships are as they should be. I am called to happiness by being a maker of peace. This is far more positive than the absence of trouble or war. As with any problem, if we are not a part of the solution, there is a strong possibility that we are part of the problem. We may not be able to bring about global peace, but we can certainly work toward creating peace in the lives of those with whom we come into contact.

To Think About
Who is awaiting my outstretched hand of reconciliation?

Prayer
Lord, let your peace on earth begin with me. Amen.

"Your light must shine before others."
(Matthew 5:16)

August

18

Background
Jesus has just told his disciples that they are "the salt of the earth" and "the light of the world." They are to bring a wholesome flavor to society by the way they live, and thus set an example that will guide others to a deeper commitment to God. The glory that will arise, of course, will be for God's greater glory, not their own.

Reflection
There is nothing more beautiful than those who are goodness incarnate. The last thing they seek is praise or glory for themselves. They act like mirrors that reflect God's love to others, and they reflect the praise of others to God. At the heart of their goodness lies the conviction that they are but instruments chosen by God for the building of his kingdom.

To Think About
Wherever I go this day, I can be a reflection God's love.

Prayer
Lord, though I am weak, use me as your instrument of love. Amen.

August

19

"My heart is moved with pity for the crowd."
(Mark 8:2)

Background
Mark has already told us of the feeding of a multitude of Jews (see Mark 6:35-44). Now in this account, Gentiles are fed and thereby assured that they, too, are invited to be part of the story of salvation. The disciples are invited to help in the nourishing of the Gentiles, for the mission of Jesus is to all people. The story bears a strong resemblance to the Last Supper and is a promise of the eucharist banquet.

Reflection
People who have worldly wealth seldom experience physical hunger. As their physical hunger decreases, however, their spiritual hunger often increases. Wealth does not always bring happiness; in fact, it often brings the opposite. The ideal is to have enough to live on—and enough to share. The most difficult lesson we have to learn in life, of course, is to know when we have enough.

To Think About
It is often easier to judge when others have enough than it is to judge when I have enough.

Prayer
Lord, may my wants be few and my friends many.
Amen.

"But whoever obeys and teaches these command-ments will be called greatest in the kingdom of heaven." (Matthew 5:19)

August
20

Background

For the orthodox Jew in Jesus' day, religion involves keeping thousands of small rules. For them, their eternal salvation depends on how well they keep these regulations. In an effort to make his message more meaningful and life-giving, Jesus reduces the whole code of law to a few simple directives. Is it any wonder that he becomes a threat to the establish-ment?

Reflection

We are told that an ounce of example is worth a ton of advice. Before we can dare to teach we must show, by our obedience to God's commands, that we are endeavoring to practice what we preach. Through obedience we, like the branch of the vine, are rooted in Jesus Christ and he is able to bear fruit through us. We must not worry; rather, we must remain one with Christ and trust that he will give the increase as he sees fit.

To Think About

God can do great things through those who are willing to work anonymously.

Prayer

Lord, to thee be all the honor and glory. Amen.

August

21

"... if ... your brother has anything against you ... go first and be reconciled." (Matthew 5:23-24)

Background
When a Jew of Jesus' day becomes estranged from God, a sacrifice is needed to heal the broken relationship. Sacrifice, however, can never atone for what the Jews refer to as "the sin of a high hand," that is a sin that has been deliberately committed. The Jewish principle also teaches that for a sacrifice to be effective, confession and true repentance are necessary so that any damage can be undone.

Reflection
The path to God always leads through our brothers and sisters. When we celebrate Eucharist, when we come to offer our sacrifice to God, we are expressing and seeking unity and communion with God. The only prerequisite is that we hold nothing against a brother or sister. Before we can hope to be at one with God, we must first be at one with those about us.

To Think About
To forgive is to set another free and to be freed in the process.

Prayer
Lord, show me those I need to forgive the most, and help me to forgive them. Amen.

"If your right eye causes you to sin, tear it out."
(Matthew 5:29)

August

22

Background
Behind the Jewish concept of sin lies the notion of a piece of cord stretched across a pathway, deliberately positioned to make one stumble. Jesus does not mean that we literally tear out our eye; rather, he means that we should be prepared to go to any length to ensure that the cause of sin within our lives is removed, no matter the cost.

Reflection
Is it our eyes or our ears that cause the greatest problems in life? The sight of another's wealth so often causes envy; the news of another's good fortune often gives rise to feelings of jealousy and resentment. Yet, the heart is the true eye of the soul. If we can set our hearts on living the kind of life Jesus invites us to enjoy, many of our problems will cease to exist.

To Think About
May I try to see things from Jesus' perspective this day.

Prayer
Lord, create within me a new heart so that I may see. Amen.

August

23

"Let your 'Yes' mean 'Yes' and your 'No' mean 'No.'" (Matthew 5:37)

Background
The need for oath taking is a consequence of humankind's sinfulness. It depicts untruthfulness and distrust of neighbor, against which the oath is thought to protect others. In the lifestyle being taught by Jesus, there is no need for oaths because truthfulness is guaranteed by the very integrity of the person.

Reflection
One of the greatest treats in life is to meet a person who is transparent, i.e., someone in whom there is no guile, no hidden agenda—someone who is honest. When we are dealing with such a person, we feel like we're encountering a rare beauty. In our desire to be accepted, or fearing that we might offend the feelings of another, we often say one thing but mean another. Honesty, on the other hand, is the fruit of many choices, minute by minute, to say and do the truth regardless of the consequences.

To Think About
Persons are as good as their word.

Prayer
Lord, may the words of my mouth mirror the desires of my heart. Amen.

"It is like a mustard seed that, when it is sown in the ground, is the smallest of all the seeds on the earth." (Mark 4:31)

Background
In Palestine at the time of Jesus, a mustard seed represents the smallest thing imaginable. Tiny though it is, it grows to be nine or ten feet tall. Because the small black seeds are particularly appealing to birds, it is quite common for a mustard tree to be covered with birds and their nests.

Reflection
A person introduced evangelist Dwight Moody to a woman by saying, "This is ___, a woman of great faith." The woman responded, "No, I am a woman of little faith but with a great God." When we realize how great our God is, our faith becomes unshakable. No matter what might happen, we know that God will not abandon us.

To Think About
"And behold, I am with you always, until the end of the age." (Matthew 28:20)

Prayer
Lord, may I never take my eyes from you. Amen.

August

24

August

25

"If anyone wants to go to law with you over your tunic, hand him your cloak as well." *(Matthew 5:40)*

Background
The Israelites are descended from the Semites, for whom the law of vengeance is foremost—a law that leads to constant strife and innumerable crimes. Throughout the early history of the chosen people, the law of retaliation is recognized as an integral part of their ethical code. Jesus' notion of forgiveness, however, is ethically light years ahead of what the Israelites were used to.

Reflection
Victor Hugo, in *Les Miserables,* tells of how Jean Valjean served nineteen years in prison for stealing a loaf of bread. On his release, Valjean made his way to the home of an elderly bishop who gave him supper and a bed for the night. Valjean then stole the bishop's silver plates and ran off. When arrested, both he and the plates were brought to the bishop, whose only reply was: "I gave them to him." The bishop then said to Valjean: "You forgot to take these candlesticks." The bishop's act changed the man's life.

To Think About
Possessions are gifts when used for others.

Prayer
Lord, may my possessions be used as seeds for an eternal harvest. Amen.

"But I say this to you, love your enemies, and pray for those who persecute you." (Matthew 5:44)

Background
There are four words for "love" in the Greek language, and each one expresses a different kind of love. There is the noun *storge*, which refers to family love; there is *eros,* which describes the passionate feelings of lovers; there is *philia,* which is the love a person has for a dear friend; and there is *agape,* which denotes unimaginable benevolence and good will. *Agape* is used in this passage.

Reflection
The preacher called for a time of reflection, asked the congregation to think about their worst enemies, and invited everyone to forgive these persons. Finally, he called the congregation to release their enemies to God. At that moment, an elderly man called out from the back pew: "Wait a minute! I'm still counting all my enemies!" The older we get, the more persons we need to forgive, and when we fail to love an enemy we are held prisoners by our enmity.

To Think About
Loving an enemy is giving love for no reason.

Prayer
Lord, help me to deal with my enemies as you would. Amen.

August

27

". . . so that your almsgiving may be secret. And your father who sees in secret will repay you."
(Matthew 6:4)

Background

Although the notion of almsgiving is not found in the Old Testament, it appears repeatedly in the New. Mosaic legislation tends to promote almsgiving in the spirit of charity and for prevention of destitution among the people. The Pharisees are ostentatious in their almsgiving. A regard to the state of the poor and needy is enjoined as a Christian duty, a duty that is not neglected by the early Christians.

Reflection

When we find it difficult to pinpoint the outstanding quality in a person, we sometimes say that the person's heart is in "the right place." This means that the person is well intentioned. Because it is impossible for us to read the heart of another, it is thus impossible for us to judge. Only God knows the heart's intentions and, consequently, only God can judge and reward. When we do things secretly for another, they're done for God.

To Think About

What I give in secret is stored in the heavenly bank.

Prayer

Lord, may I use your temporal gifts for their eternal purpose. Amen.

"In praying, do not babble like the pagans, who think that they will be heard because of their many words." (Matthew 6:7)

August
28

Background
The Jews have standard prayers that are uttered at certain fixed times each day. Devout Jews stop wherever they are—unless the place is "unclean," of course—and recite the prayers in a standing position. Needless to say, the Pharisees delight in being able to publicly demonstrate their piety by seeking the most public place for the recitation of their prayers.

Reflection
There is nothing that can dissipate the strength of the human spirit more quickly than a chatterbox, i.e., someone who talks relentlessly. As sleep refreshes the body, so silence refreshes the spirit. In true prayer there is need for few words—in fact, only four: "Thy will be done." When silence enters our prayer, we rest with God. It's no wonder that silence is deemed to be the language of lovers.

To Think About
The fruit of silence is prayer. The fruit of payer is faith. The fruit of faith is love. (Mother Teresa)

Prayer
Lord, still the urgings of my heart so that my spirit may rest in you. Amen.

August

29

"From within people, from their hearts, come evil thoughts." (Mark 7:21)

Background

Jesus is always critical of the attitudes of those leaders within the community who seek to reduce the keeping of the Law to a series of human rules and regulations. He appeals to his hearers to understand that human goodness, or morality, is not a matter of external conformity to laws or traditions. Rather, morality concerns itself with how one is at heart.

Reflection

Apart from those actions that are governed by the body's autonomic nervous system, our actions begin as thoughts within our minds. In *Paradise Lost,* John Milton writes: "The mind is its own place and in itself it can make a heaven of hell or a hell of heaven." If we control our thoughts, we control our lives. By controlling our thoughts we can bring heaven a little closer to earth and earth a little closer to heaven.

To Think About

"Where your treasure is, there also will your heart be." (Matthew 6:21)

Prayer

Lord, cleanse the thoughts of my heart by the inspiration of your Holy Spirit. Amen.

The woman . . . begged him to drive the demon out of her daughter. (Mark 7:26)

August
30

Background
Demons are considered to be spiritual beings who are at enmity with God and have certain powers over humans. They are said to belong to that group of angels that "kept not their first estate," who are "unclean spirits," "fallen angels," the angels of the devil (see Matthew 25:41; Revelation 12:7-9). The Phoenician woman in this story recognizes that Jesus has the power and so she does not hesitate to ask.

Reflection
Pope Paul VI wrote that "the intrinsic characteristic of prayer is trust . . . It is no longer a voice crying in the darkness, but is a real dialogue, and a response not only to a divine precept but also to a promise. 'Pray and your prayers will be heard.'" Often, all that is lacking in our prayer is perseverance. We cease praying because we do not get an immediate answer.

To Think About
The best aid to prayer, however, is stout working. (Thomas Carlyle)

Prayer
Thank you, Father, for hearing my prayer. Amen.

August

31

"For where your treasure is, there also will your heart be." *(Matthew 6:21)*

Background

According to the Bible, the heart is the center of not only spiritual activity but of all the operations of human life. "Heart" and "soul," in fact, are used interchangeably. The process of salvation begins in the heart by the open reception of the love of God, while the rejection of that love hardens the heart. What we value will ultimately dictate how we live our lives.

Reflection

So often people pray to get to heaven and forget that their mission is to bring heaven on earth. When our talents are used to build a heaven about us, we experience a heaven on earth. No wealth can ever replace the joy of knowing that we are doing all within our power to better the lot of others. It is in this way that we incarnate the Prayer "Thy kingdom come."

To Think About

There are no pockets in the death shroud.

Prayer

Thy kingdom come both within me and through me. Amen.

"But seek first the kingdom [of God] and his righteousness, and all these things will be given you besides." (Matthew 6:33)

Background
Jesus is gently leading his hearers to the point where he will tell them that they are not to worry (v. 34). Worry stems from a distrust of God, with whom we are called to have a loving relationship. Worry comes from within the heart, and it often arises because we forget the past; we forget about the things that God has done for us again and again.

Reflection
An old monk was asked what his guiding light had been during his long life within the monastery. He replied: "When I was a novice, I made a simple rule for myself. Before doing anything, I would ask: 'Is this what God would want me to do?' If the answer was 'yes' then I would do it; if not, I would refrain. I could never even begin to explain the happiness I've known in keeping that rule."

To Think About
If God's plan is for my happiness, I couldn't do better than to follow it.

Prayer
Lord, may I learn to love your law. Amen.

September

1

September

2

"Whoever believes in me will never thirst."
(John 6:35)

Background

We do not do justice to Jesus' message if we take at
face value many of the things he shared. This is
especially true when we reflect on the parables or on
Jesus' sayings, where we find several layers of meaning. This quotation is a good example. The thirst
that Jesus has in mind is something far deeper than
mere physical thirst; it is the longing of the heart
that only God can satisfy.

Reflection

If we are honest with ourselves we have to admit to a
thirst within us that can never be touched by anything human. We may try to satiate this thirst by
accumulating possessions or by becoming hyperac-
tive with various activities and distractions. But this
thirst is for God and only God can quench it.

To Think About

… for you my soul thirsts, Like a land parched, life-
less, and without water. (Psalm 63:2)

Prayer

Lord, I thirst. Amen.

"Teacher, do you not care that we are perishing?"
(Mark 4:38)

Background
The Sea of Galilee is famous for its sudden storms. Within minutes, perfectly calm waters can be transformed into raging seas. Wind coming from the plateaus of Trachonitis and Mount Hermon are funneled into the lake by means of ravines on the northeastern front.

Reflection
One night a man dreamed that he was walking along the beach with the Lord, when across the sky flashed scenes from his life. In most scenes he noticed two sets of footprints in the sand. One set belonged to him and the other to the Lord. After the last scene, the man realized that at times there was only one set of footprints. "You promised that if I followed you, you would never abandon me. However, I notice that during the most turbulent times of my life, there was only one set of footprints. Where were you?" The Lord replied: "When you saw only one set of footprints, my child, that was when I carried you."

To Think About
Faith is daring the spirit to go on when the eyes can no longer see.

Prayer
Lord, strengthen my trust in you. Amen.

September

4

"*Do to others whatever you would have them do to you.*" *(Matthew 7:12)*

Background

This mandate is not unique to the Judaic literature. When Rabbi Hillel was challenged by a proselyte to stand on one foot and explain the whole of the Law, Hillel did so and responded: "That which displeases you, do not do to another. This is the whole Law; the rest is merely commentary." The fact that the command as found in Matthew is couched in the affirmative is of no real consequence.

Reflection

So often we find that we react to others rather than respond to them. The difference between the two involves the thought process. A reaction is automatic and demands little if any thought, whereas a response presupposes thoughtfulness. To treat others as we would want them to treat us necessitates that we be in control of our actions, that we allow love and forgiveness to dominate anything and everything we do.

To Think About

Good deeds are never lost; the one who plants kindness gathers love.

Prayer

Lord, may I pause before I act and realize that you are always present. Amen.

... the hand of the Lord was with him.
(Luke 1:66)

September

5

Background
This phrase is more important than it might first appear. The name, which is given at God's command, is "John," which is a shorter form of the name "Jehohanan," a name meaning "God is gracious." This passage gives us the credentials of John the Baptist and sets up the role he is to play as the forerunner of Jesus.

Reflection
We're told that youth is a gift of nature, but that old age is a work of art. What transforms the gift of nature into the work of art depends on how we use the gifts that God has given us. He has given us the gift of free will, whereby we can love him by doing what he asks. The greatest gift we can give to him— and to ourselves—is simply doing his will insofar as we know it.

To Think About
To love God is to will what He wills. (C. de Foucauld)

Prayer
Lord, as you did your Father's will, may I now do yours. Amen.

September

6

"By their fruits you will know them."
(Matthew 7:16)

Background
At the time of Jesus, the buckthorn grows in the Holy Land and produces black berries that resemble small grapes. There is also a certain thistle whose flower, when seen from a distance, resembles a fig. This causes Jesus to ask the question about getting grapes from thorns or figs from thistles. Similarly, there may be a resemblance between a true and a false prophet; it is their fruit that differentiates them.

Reflection
If we see a tree bearing apples and conclude that this is an apple tree, we don't expect to be awarded a degree in botany. This is true in the life of a Christian; the fruit of one's life distinguishes a disciple of Jesus. With our cooperation, the Holy Spirit that was given to us as gift at our baptism can bring about beautiful fruit this very day, if we allow him.

To Think About
God is waiting for my permission to use me.

Prayer
Lord, make something beautiful for yourself out of my life. Amen.

"Not everyone who says to me, 'Lord, Lord,' will enter the kingdom of heaven, but only the one who does the will of my Father." (Matthew 7:21)

September 7

Background

The expression "Lord, Lord" is an integral part of the life of the members of early Church. It amounts to mere words, however, unless it is founded on love. Paul says that no matter what gifts a person might have, they are useless without the gift of love. For Matthew, the test of belonging to the kingdom is in doing the will of the Father.

Reflection

An army functions on obedience. While initiative is encouraged, actions must serve the good of all. If each person does what he or she feels is best, the safety of all is endangered. Working for God is somewhat the same. He will use us in the best possible way if we but trust him. We may not see the relevance of what he asks, of course; only time will disclose this.

To Think About

God knows where he is leading me.

Prayer

May my one desire be to do your will. Amen.

September

8

"Lord, if you wish, you can make me clean."
(Matthew 8:2)

Background
At the time of Jesus, lepers are stoned if they approach an orthodox scribe or rabbi. The Greek verb that describes the approach of the leper is *proskunein,* which is used only when speaking of "the worship of the gods." The leper's whole approach is to imply that he knows he is in the presence of a man of God.

Reflection
"Let go and let God." This is hard to do because we are afraid of what will happen if we entrust ourselves completely to God. As we progress in a life of prayer, however, our petition gradually becomes: "Thy will be done." We move from serving God as advisors to where we, like Mary, want everything to be done "according to thy word." It is then that God is most powerful in our lives.

To Think About
I can give my troubles to God. He will not wish to sleep anyway.

Prayer
Lord, if you wish, you can make me clean. Amen.

He touched her hand, the fever left her, and she rose and waited on him. (Matthew 8:15)

Background
At the synagogue Jesus cures the man who was possessed by a demon. Then, on his way home, Jesus cures the centurion's servant. Because of the effort involved in working these miracles, Jesus is tired. For him, however, human need is always of paramount importance, and so Peter's mother-in-law is cured without a second thought.

Reflection
Health has many definitions. One that is particularly appealing is: "Health is the ability to be of service to oneself and others." In Peter's mother-in-law, we have a model of all genuine healing. Jesus comes into contact with the woman, the woman is cured and, as a sign of the cure, she ministers to others. When Jesus touches us, through the gift of good health, wealth, or whatever, we must in turn touch others with the blessings we have received.

To Think About
Love of God is an endless desire to give of oneself to others.

Prayer
Lord, may I be supple in your hands. Amen.

September

10

"*Whatever place does not welcome you or listen to you, leave there and shake the dust off your feet.*" *(Mark 6:11)*

Background

Hospitality is a sacred duty in the East. In fact, it is not the duty of a stranger to search hospitality when he enters a village but the duty of the village to offer it. For the Jews, however, this hospitality goes only so far. The rabbinic law says that the dust of a Gentile country is defiled and that on returning to Palestine, a person must remove every particle of Gentile dust. Jesus makes reference to this rabbinic law when he speaks about what the disciples' response is to be if people do not listen to them.

Reflection

Various forms of the martial arts advocate that practitioners walk away from situations that could lead to violent conflict. There is often little attention given to the Christian message as it is preached. Ultimately, it is the language of love that speaks loudest. However, if having given of our best, we fail to get a hearing, we may need to move to fresh pastures.

To Think About

The less said the easier it is to mend it.
(Irish proverb)

Prayer

Lord, may I be open to all I meet and touch them with the gentleness of your love. Amen.

He went down with them and came to Nazareth, and was obedient to them. (Luke 2:51)

Background

The Scripture from which this verse is taken contains the last reference to Joseph that we find in the Gospels. We are told that, obedient to the guidance of his parents, Jesus grows to perfect manhood. It is a simple but nonetheless beautiful tribute to Joseph, who is one of the heroes who walks through the pages of the New Testament without ever uttering a word.

Reflection

We have all witnessed the scenario where a little child asks a parent, "But why must I do such-and-such?" and the parent responds, "Because I told you to." While blind obedience may have its place when we are dealing with young children, true obedience will always involve dialogue. Nobody has a monopoly on the Spirit; God's will is usually found through a common search in which people are united in mind and heart.

To Think About

Listen even to the loud and aggressive since each has his story to tell. (Max Ehrmann)

Prayer

Enable me, Lord, to listen to the many sounds of your voice. Amen.

September

12

"The one who humbles himself will be exalted."
(Luke 14:11)

Background
This parable is not so much a lesson about courtesy
or table manners as it is a commentary on who
belongs to the kingdom of God. When it comes to
entering God's kingdom, we are invited to attend.
Those who are invited are not those who are self-
sufficient but those who are lowly and recognize
their need for salvation.

Reflection
While it is difficult to be humbled, it is even more
difficult to humble oneself, since humbling oneself
necessitates dying to self and nobody wants to die.
One of the ways of humbling ourselves is by opting
for a more contemplative life and letting go of the
passing glamour of this world. It is in this way that
we make our own the words of Patrick Kavanagh:
"Let us be nothing, nothing, that God may make us
something."

To Think About
Let us lie deep in anonymous humility that God
may find us worthy material in His hands.
(P. Kavanagh)

Prayer
Lord, may I be given a true sense of what is of
lasting value. Amen.

"On the outside you appear righteous, but inside you are filled with hypocrisy and evildoing."
(Matthew 23:28)

September

13

Background
A common place for tombs at the time of Jesus is by the wayside. It is important for the Jews to avoid any contact with these tombs since to touch a tomb is to become unclean. It is the Jewish practice to white-wash all wayside tombs in preparation for the Passover. Jesus uses this practice to paint a precise picture of what the Pharisees are like: beautiful on the outside but full of rotting matter on the inside.

Reflection
Within the Western culture, so much depends on external appearances. The emphasis that is placed on presenting the right image, however, is often to the detriment of being the right person. Jesus warns us about this. He tells us that the desires of our hearts are what matters. An honest look at what our hearts desire—the values that motivate us—will tell us a lot about the direction our spiritual lives.

To Think About
Not as man sees does God see, because man sees the appearance but the Lord looks into the heart.
(1 Samuel 16:7)

Prayer
Lord, may I never forget that you see what is in my heart. Amen.

September

14

"For God did not send his Son into the world to condemn the world." (John 3:17)

Background
Jesus claims that he has come that we might have life and have it to the full (see John 10:10). We will be condemned only to the extent that we refuse to accept this life that he offers. Condemnation has little to do with being rejected by God. It is more a refusal on our part to accept the life and love he wants to share with us. We condemn ourselves!

Reflection
Jesus is the true likeness of the Father, and so he does not condemn us. Those whom the world judges to be most in need of condemnation are often those who are dearest to God. We are told that God does not have favorites but if he does, it is those who are out of favor with the powers of this world. Jesus came and gave his life, not for the self-sufficient but for the sinner.

To Think About
No pain, no palm; no thorns, no throne; . . . no cross, no crown. (W. Penn)

Prayer
By your cross and resurrection, Lord, you have set us free; you are the Savior of the world. Amen.

"Cleanse first the inside of the cup, so that the outside also may be clean." (Matthew 23:26)

September

15

Background
The Pharisees' preoccupation with cleanliness quite often borders on the ludicrous. They dread defilement in any form. The vessels mentioned here are mere metaphors for the human being. This exhortation is directed at the care that is to be taken to ensure that, while there may be external correctness, due regard of the interior disposition remains most important.

Reflection
Given that the inner disposition of a person is good, the outward expression will also be good. If the right intention is present, a person will produce the fruit that the Lord wants. Our intentions give direction to our lives.

To Think About
The heart has its reasons which reason knows nothing about. (B. Pascal)

Prayer
Lord, may the intentions of my heart be pleasing in your sight. Amen.

September

16

"If a kingdom is divided against itself, that kingdom cannot stand." (Mark 3:24)

Background
The officials at the time of Jesus never question his ability to exorcise demons, because exorcism is a common phenomenon in the East. What the officials do allege is that Jesus is in league with the devil and that it is through the power of Satan that he is able to do his exorcisms. Jesus destroys that argument, however, by pointing out that if it were true it would amount to self-destruction.

Reflection
In the "Liberty Song," John Dickinson invites the compatriots: "Then join hand in hand, brave Americans all, by uniting we stand, by dividing we fall." As with a log fire, when the logs are kept close together, the fire thrives; when the logs are spread out, it's only a matter of time before they stop burning. It is the same within any church, family, or one's personal life. Where there is togetherness there is strength.

To Think About
The strength of a chain is the strength of its weakest link.

Prayer
Lord, make me an instrument of your healing love this day. Amen.

"He took away our infirmities and bore our diseases." (Matthew 8:17)

September

17

Background
This verse is an echo of Isaiah 53:4, where we are told that the servant of the Lord bore our weaknesses and carried our sins. Jesus is called "Emmanuel," God-with-us. His birth begins the era of the Messiah, the outstanding event that the entire world of the Old Testament had been looking forward to. It is the beginning of a time of freedom, especially from the captivity of sin.

Reflection
An elderly man listened to a widow describe how her husband and children had been tragically killed in an accident and how, in spite of the best work of psychiatrists, she remained inconsolable. As he listened he began to cry, and she cried with him. She later told how that man, through his simple listening, had spoken the language of the heart and brought the healing that the most learned people had failed to bring.

To Think About
I can often do more good with a listening ear than with many words.

Prayer
Lord, create within me the willingness to accommodate others' problems. Amen.

September

18

"Whoever receives you receives me."
(Matthew 10:40)

Background
This assurance that Jesus gives to his disciples
draws on a way of speaking that is frequently used
by the Jews. They always feel that to receive a
person's deputy is the same as receiving the person.
By the same token, to refuse to receive the represen-
tative is tantamount to refusing the person who
sends the messenger.

Reflection
In an age when we try to guard our little space, and
security is so much to the fore, hospitality is all the
more important. Hospitality is basically about
letting people into our hearts and allowing them to
be different, thereby accepting them for what and
who they are. When we make the effort to be hos-
pitable, we say: "You're all right!" In this way, we
enable others to be the best people they can be.

To Think About
Those who give when they are asked have waited
too long.

Prayer
Remove the blinders from my eyes, Lord, that I may
see you in everyone I meet. Amen.

"Courage, child, your sins are forgiven."
(Matthew 9:2)

September

19

Background
In Palestine at the time of Jesus, it is believed that all sickness is the result of sin and that a cure can only take place once the sin has been forgiven. Because of this, it is important for sick persons to believe that their sin has been forgiven in order that the path can be cleared for healing to take place. This is an instance of where a healthy mind is a prerequisite for a healthy body.

Reflection
Complimentary medicine adopts a holistic approach and maintains that healing happens from the inside out—from the more important organs of the body to the lesser ones. When Jesus forgives the sins of the paralytic, the way is clear for a physical healing to take place. For each of us individually, it may be that there is some illness within that has its origin in a sin that has yet to be forgiven.

To Think About
America's present need is not heroics, but healing. (W. G. Harding)

Prayer
Jesus, I open myself to the healing wholeness you offer. Heal me if it be your will. Amen.

September

20

"I desire mercy, not sacrifice." (Matthew 9:13)

Background

A more precise translation of this passage is: "I desire mercy more than sacrifice" (see also Hosea 6:6). Jesus is not saying that sacrifices are unacceptable but that every sacrifice we offer should be motivated by love and should come from the heart. A sacrifice that is just the mere performance of an empty ritual is just that—empty!

Reflection

Mercy is what we give to another; sacrifice is what we give to God. Because we go to God through our neighbors, we must first say "I love you" to our neighbors before we can say it to God. In fact, one of the shortest routes to God is through our neighbors. Time and again Jesus equates himself with the neighbor.

To Think About

Each loving act says loud and clear: "I love you, God loves you; I care, God cares."

Prayer

Give me the openness, Lord, which will enable me to discover what is really important. Amen.

"People do not put new wine into old wineskins."
(Matthew 9:17)

September

21

Background
Jesus is calling for an openness of mind, whereby his listeners are prepared to consider new ideas and new values for living. Among the religious values of his time, there is a resentment for anything that is new. It is this hostility that eventually leads to his being rejected and crucified. He realizes that when anything human stops growing, it starts dying.

Reflection
One of the most difficult tasks confronting any preacher is to move people from being good to becoming great. People often become so comfortable with leading a good life that they are unwilling to let go of the sure and the tried. The message that Jesus comes to bring requires that we hear it as if for the first time and act on it as if it were the only thing that matters.

To Think About
It often takes more faith to say "I will" than "I can."

Prayer
That I might let go of what is good, O Lord, for what is great. Amen.

September

22

"Go and do likewise." *(Luke 10:37)*

Background
This verse is part of the story about the Good Samaritan, which takes place on the road between Jerusalem and Jericho. This road is perched almost 2,300 feet above sea level at Jerusalem, and drops 3,600 feet over a twenty-mile stretch, until it reaches Jericho, which is 1,300 feet below sea level. As a winding, twisting road, it is ideal for robbers because it provides both cover and the opportunity of a quick getaway.

Reflection
The gospel is a call to action. The one who is a neighbor to the one who is mugged is not one who preaches by word but by action. Our most effective pulpit will be the pulpit of our lives. The only language our fellow pilgrims may understand is the language of our actions. Ultimately, the gospel rarely needs much of an explanation when it is lived.

To Think About
No one would remember the Good Samaritan if he'd only had good intentions. (M. Thatcher)

Prayer
May the gospel that I preach find an echo in the life I lead. Amen.

"If your right eye causes you to sin, tear it out and throw it away." (Matthew 5:29)

September

23

Background

The word for "to sin," in this context, is *skandalon,* which is a form of the word *skandalethron* and refers to the stick in a trap on which bait is hung. It is this stick that leads to an animal's own destruction. The word as it is used here implies anything that might bring about a person's own destruction.

Reflection

John of the Cross tells us that whether a bird is held by a chain or a thread, it still cannot fly. In our effort to become united to Jesus, we have to be prepared to remove even the slightest sin or obstacle. God will not settle until he is Lord of all of our lives. He will not settle for anything less than our all.

To Think About

In whatever you do, remember your last days, and you will never sin. (Sirach 7:36)

Prayer

May I appreciate that in having you, Lord, I have everything. Amen.

September

24

"There is need of only one thing." (Luke 10:42)

Background

Jesus is visiting Mary and Martha "on his way to Jerusalem." For Luke, this brief phrase has a special significance: Jesus is on his way to die. Caught up in the turmoil of trying to decide between his will and that of the Father—the battle of bending his will to the Father's—Jesus just needs space and time to come to terms with what lies ahead.

Reflection

For those who are in love with Jesus, all things speak of him. He colors their thoughts, their desires, their plans. These people can do the work of a Martha but it is done with a special quality that sets it apart. They try to discover what God wants of them and then they are prepared to do it with all their strength—even if it is something as simple and profound as sitting and listening!

To Think About

The secret of being in love is to be lovely; the secret of being lovely is being unselfish.

Prayer

Fill me with your love, dear God, so that I can do the ordinary in an extraordinary way. Amen.

"Teacher, we wish to see a sign from you."
(Matthew 12:38)

September

25

Background
The Jews always ask for marvelous signs of those who claim to be messengers from God. For them, a sign indicates something fantastic. Unfortunately, the Jews expect to see God in only the extraordinary—and fail to realize that God is seen more clearly in the ordinary, everyday events of life.

Reflection
Living at a time when the TV presents us with a new image every few seconds, we can easily become preoccupied with looking for fascinating stimuli. As a result, we are in danger of failing to see the reality of God's presence that exists under our very noses. Without time and thought, we become blind to what lies beneath and within the ordinary. Yet, it is the ordinary that speaks to us of the silent presence of God.

To Think About
The only thing greater than the wonders of nature is my awareness of them.

Prayer
May I have a heart that is questing, O Lord, and a soul that is resting. Amen.

"Everyone who asks, receives; and the one who seeks, finds; and to the one who knocks, the door will be opened." (Luke 11:10)

Background

Jesus is not teaching us what prayer is but how we should pray. One of the essential ingredients of prayer is trusting perseverance. We keep praying, not that we hope to change God's will but rather, that we might bring our will into conformity with God's, trusting that we will be given what he knows to be for our good.

Reflection

We may sometimes wonder why our prayers are not answered. We are promised that if we ask, we will receive; if we seek, we will find; if we knock, the door will be opened for us. However, we are not told what we will receive or what we will find or what will be awaiting us when the door is opened! All we know for certain is that whatever awaits us will be the best we can possibly receive.

To Think About

Prayer is not a vain attempt to change God's will; it is a filial desire to learn God's will and to share it. (G. Buttrick)

Prayer

Lord, teach me to knock—and teach me to wait. Amen.

"Do not think that I have come to abolish the law or the prophets." (Matthew 5:17)

September

27

Background
This defense of what the Jews call the "Law" is rather unusual for Jesus who, time and again, breaks it. The Law refers to any of four different things: the Ten Commandments, the first five books of the Bible, the whole of Scripture, or the oral or scribal Law. In the time of Jesus, the last meaning is the most common—and it was this that he abhorred.

Reflection
Reading the Gospels is like peeling an onion. Each time we prayerfully read them, we become aware of a deeper layer and perhaps "stronger" meaning. Quite often we are confronted and challenged by an aspect of Christian living that we had never thought of before. Jesus comes that we might have life and have it to the full. One of the primary ways in which he draws us to deeper levels of life is through the gospel call.

To Think About
Time can either make a law more precious or render it impractical.

Prayer
Lord, may I treasure the wisdom of the ages. Amen.

September

28

> "Blessed are the meek." (Matthew 5:5)

Background

The Greek word for "meek" is *praus,* which does not have any of the subservient connotations we associate with the word today. Aristotle's custom was to define any virtue as the halfway point between two extremes. Meekness lays between excessive anger and too little anger. A more accurate translation of the text would be: "Blessed are those who are angry at the right time."

Reflection

Our basic instinct is for self-preservation. When we are confronted by another, we may feel threatened and, consequently, will defend ourselves by erecting whatever barrier we can find. When we are treated with meekness, however, our barriers come down and we melt like ice before the sun. Ultimately, it is gentle meekness that becomes the perfume of many memories.

To Think About

A spoonful of sugar often helps the medicine go down.

Prayer

Lord, help me to think before I act. Amen.

"Whoever eats my flesh and drinks my blood remains in me and I in him." (John 6:56)

Background
For the Jewish mentality, blood belongs to God because it stands for the very essence of life. This is why a true Jew will not eat meat that has not been completely drained of blood (see Deuteronomy 15:23). Jesus is inviting his followers to make him the very source of their lives. In light of this, we can understand how the one who drinks the blood of Jesus will never die.

Reflection
Time and again we may wonder what effect our reception of the body and blood of Jesus has in our lives. Bear in mind that what is most important is often not visible to the eye. Thus the work Jesus is doing within us is often silent and hidden—and he will achieve whatever he wants, in his own way and in his own time.

To Think About
To be immortal is to share in Divinity.
(Saint Clement of Alexandria)

Prayer
May I never allow myself to be separated from you, O Lord. Amen.

They returned to Jerusalem to look for him.
(Luke 2:45)

Background

During the time of the Passover, it is the custom for the Sanhedrin to meet in the Temple court to publicly discuss various theological questions. When Joseph and Mary discover that Jesus is missing, they return to Jerusalem and find him listening to and participating in the discussions at the Temple.

Reflection

For the spirit-filled person, God is found everywhere. All of creation speaks of his presence. Saint Bernard said that we will find something far greater in the woods than we will in books. Stones and trees, he maintained, are capable of teaching us what we can never learn from masters. If we hope to see God in the most insignificant, we must first learn to slow down and become inwardly still.

To Think About

The heavens proclaim the glory of God.

Prayer

Close the eyes of my mind, O Lord, that you may open the eyes of my soul. Amen.

October

1

> *"The kingdom of heaven is like a net thrown into the sea, which collects fish of every kind."*
> *(Matthew 13:47)*

Background

There are two ways of fishing in Palestine in the time of Jesus. One way is to throw a handheld net into the sea and drag it to shore. The other is by means of the square trawl net that is pulled around behind a boat. As the boat moves, the net forms a cone shape and fish are swept into the cone.

Reflection

The net thrown into the sea of life is often compared to the love of God that captures all of us. We are equally and infinitely loved by the Father. When we can realize that each person we meet is a brother or sister, regardless of color, creed, or history, we are beginning to live within the kingdom of heaven.

To Think About

Some people make the world more special just by being in it.

Prayer

Lord, may I recognize you amidst the brokenness of humanity. Amen.

October

2

"Give to the one who asks of you, and do not turn your back on one who wants to borrow."
(Matthew 5:42)

Background

According to Jewish law, giving can never be refused, and certain principles govern the way in which the giving should be done. It has to be done in private, for example, and the giver should not know the person to whom the gift is given. What is given has to be beneficial to the recipient and all forms of giving are seen as giving to God.

Reflection

We often fail to appreciate the fact that we will leave life the same way we entered it; with no possessions. Yet, between birth and death, we spend so much time and energy amassing possessions and building empires. Possessions are gifts to be shared with others. If we hold on to anything, it dies with us; if we give it to someone in need, it goes before us to become part of our treasure in heaven.

To Think About

My true wealth can be measured by the paucity of my needs.

Prayer

Lord, may I learn what is important in life. Amen.

"This is my beloved Son; listen to him."
(Mark 9:7b)

October

3

Background
This is a paraphrase of Isaiah 42:1 and presents
Jesus as a suffering servant. The passage gives the
three disciples a glimpse of who Jesus is—an image
that will be a source of strength for them when the
rejection and suffering of the passion begins.

Reflection
Love changes everything. People do strange things
when they know they are loved. In the same way,
people will do almost anything for someone they
love. Because Jesus knows that he is loved by the
Father, he gives himself completely to the Father's
work. He tells us: "As the Father has loved me, so I
have loved you" (John 15:9). If we really believe
Jesus, imagine what the consequences might be!

To Think About
If I were the only child that God my Father ever created, he couldn't love me any more.

Prayer
Jesus, let me experience the Father's love. Amen.

October

4

"Everyone who looks at a woman with lust has already committed adultery with her in his heart." (Matthew 5:28)

Background

The Jewish rabbis have a saying: "The eyes and the hand are the two brokers of sin." Also: "Eye and heart are the two handmaids of sin." The lustful gaze is mentioned time and again in the rabbinical literature, and is reprobated with scarcely less vigor than we find in this gospel passage. Jesus is stressing the fact that there is an eternal desire of which adultery is only the fruit.

Reflection

Jesus always presents us with the ideal. The fact that we fail to live up to the ideal is not because it is impossible to achieve, but because we are still struggling with a human nature that so often inclines us to sin. We must never forget that we are not ready-made saints who are in danger of losing our sanctity, but sinners who sometimes get led astray. Of ourselves, we can do nothing; with Christ, all things are possible.

To Think About

Victory lies more in the effort than in the achieving.

Prayer

May your will be done both in me, God, and by me. Amen.

"You are worth more than many sparrows."
(Matthew 10:31)

Background
In Jesus' time, when people purchase four sparrows, they are given five; one is thrown in for "good measure." Because of this, that fifth sparrow is seen to have no value whatsoever. Matthew tells us that God, who cares even for the sparrow that has no value in the eyes of humankind, will care for us who are of much greater value.

Reflection
In his book *Song of the Bird,* Anthony de Mello tells the following story: "God decided to visit the earth and sent an angel to survey the situation prior to his visit. The angel returned with his report. 'Most of them lack food,' he said, 'and many of them lack employment.' God said: 'Then I shall become incarnate in the form of food for the hungry and work for the unemployed.'" God then created you and me!

To Think About
Providence begins with attention to others, with an act of gracious self-forgetting.

Prayer
May I learn to give, O Lord, without counting the cost. Amen.

October

6

"Stop judging." (Matthew 7:1)

Background

To judge is not simply to have an opinion; we cannot avoid this. Rather "judging," as the word is used here, refers to harsh assessment. Jesus is always quick to condemn any malicious judgments we make about someone's behavior, feelings, or motives. The ways of the world would say: "Think badly and you will not be far wrong." This is far from what Jesus teaches.

Reflection

Aristotle had a profound insight into what it means to be a human being. He said that "our feelings towards our friends reflect our feelings towards ourselves." Nowhere is this seen more clearly than in the exercise of judgment. Our hidden faults are often clearly reflected in those about us. When we learn to accept the little child that lies within us, we will learn to accept the children of God about us.

To Think About

Blind men should judge no colors. (J. Heywood)

Prayer

Lord, may I never forget that my vocation is to help; to you alone belongs judgment. Amen.

"I have much more to tell you, but you cannot bear it now." (John 16:12)

October

7

Background
Jesus knows the human condition. He knows that time and again we are incapable of understanding things we hear. Even now, at the end of his public life, Jesus tells his disciples that there are many other things he needs to tell them. Only when the Holy Spirit comes, however, will they be capable of comprehending these things.

Reflection
Many people live according to what fortunetellers predict for them. In his wisdom, however, God does not show us the crosses that lie ahead of us, for we would probably reject them and thereby fail to partake in his master plan. Just as the Trinity embodies the Father, the Son, and the Holy Spirit, the crosses of life involve their own threesome: the human person, the problem, and Jesus.

To Think About
It is the prayer of suffering that saves the world. (Saint Mary of Jesus)

Prayer
May the Father, Son, and Holy Spirit walk with me this day. Amen.

October

8

... and [Jesus] did not need anyone to testify about human nature. He himself understood it well. (John 2:25)

Background

Many follow Jesus because of the wonders they witness him performing, and nobody knows this better than Jesus himself. He knows that there are many who will acclaimed him as Messiah without appreciating the kind of messiahship he has in mind. Knowing the fickleness of human nature, Jesus is careful not to allow his mission to be hijacked for mere human goals.

Reflection

"There is so much good in the worst of us and so much bad in the best of us that it ill behooves the best of us to say anything about the worst of us." While at first this old saying might appear to be a tongue-twister, it speaks a profound truth. Only Jesus knows how great the individual is, and we can never dare to view another from the outside.

To Think About

How often do I attempt to play God by trying to create another in my own image and likeness?

Prayer

Lord, that I might see. Amen.

Jesus said to them, "Come, have breakfast."
(John 21:12)

October

9

Background
After the resurrection, Jesus understands the difficulty his disciples are experiencing and thus attempts to show the reality of what has happened by using common everyday events. When he appears to his disciples and they still find it difficult to believe, he shows them his hands and side. In this instance, he teaches by cooking a simple meal for them.

Reflection
The root meaning of the word "companionship" is "a sharing of bread with someone." Perhaps each day we share food with others and take its significance for granted. When we decide to share a meal, we commit ourselves to loyalty, support and, above all, courtesy in the way we treat those with whom we eat. When we come to appreciate the sanctity of the "ordinary," we grow to reverence the "sacred."

To Think About
The grace of God is to be found in courtesy.

Prayer
Thank you, Lord, for the privilege of being able to feed others with the life of your love. Amen.

October

10

"*But woe to you who are rich, for you have received your consolation.*" (Luke 6:24)

Background

The "rich" are those who seek to accumulate possessions—lawfully or otherwise. It isn't riches in themselves that Jesus condemns but rather, seeing in those riches the source of happiness. Riches are meant to free us to serve those who are less fortunate. They are not meant to imprison us by binding us.

Reflection

The greatest part of acquiring something is often the anticipation, for no sooner do we receive something than we find that its charm begins to fade. Our hearts hunger to be filled with the goodness of God. By setting our hearts on acquiring possessions, we may numb this hunger, but only temporarily; it will return greater than ever.

To Think About

A person is as wealthy as the scarcity of their needs.

Prayer

You are all I need, O Lord. Amen.

"Rather, new wine must be poured into fresh wineskins." (Luke 5:38)

October

11

Background
Before the invention of glass and bottles, wine was kept in wineskins. When new, the skins were able to expand a little. As they grew older they became harder and more unyielding. When the wine was fermenting, it gave off gases that a new wineskin would be able to accommodate because of its flexibility. If the wine were to be placed in old skins, the old skins would burst and both wine and container would be lost.

Reflection
There is something beautiful about the "known"; it makes us feel secure and in command. Change, however, brings fear of the unknown as we let go of that which is familiar. The word of God, as encountered in the Gospels, is ever ancient and yet ever new. It calls upon us to travel through uncharted waters. The only lifeline we are given is Jesus' assurance: "I am with you always" (Matthew 28:20).

To Think About
Where do I feel threatened by the challenge of the gospel?

Prayer
Lord, empty me of what is "me" so that you can fill me with all that is "you." Amen.

"The sabbath was made for man, not man for the sabbath." (Mark 2:27)

Background

Work on the Sabbath day is forbidden. "Work" is classified under almost forty different headings, two of which are reaping and threshing. The disciples, therefore, are lawbreakers according to the Law. To the Jewish rabbis of the time, this is a matter of deadly sin, whereas Jesus makes the point that the universal law of love is the only one that really matters.

Reflection

Although we do, indeed, need "law," there is a security to it that can lead us to a sense of righteousness. For example, those of us who go to church regularly may be tempted to have a low regard for those who don't. Yet, gong to church is meaningless if it does not enable us to become more loving people. At the end of our days we will be judged on how well we have loved, not on how well we have kept the law— secular law or temporal law.

To Think About

Where in my life do I need to be more vigilant in observing the law of love?

Prayer

Lord, may I be small enough to recognize my need for law and big enough to know when to lay it aside. Amen.

"You are the light of the world." (Matthew 5:14)

October

13

Background
Here we find him Jesus using a familiar metaphor, which he often does. In this metaphor, he refers to his disciples in terms of "light." Most of the peasant Palestinian houses have just one room and this is where the family eats and sleeps. Because the house is so small, only one lamp is needed to provide light for the entire house. If the light goes out, of course, there is total darkness.

Reflection
Instead of being mighty spotlights, our lives are more like candles that burn silently. Although a candle does not threaten, it does contain the lethal power to destroy. When times become dark, the candle has the power to gather people together. The darker the surrounding world, the more brightly the candle shines, giving comfort and assurance to all.

To Think About
I am called to be God's light to this world.

Prayer
May others come to know you, O Lord, through the light of my life. Amen.

October

14

"Unless your righteousness surpasses that of the scribes and Pharisees, you will not enter into the kingdom of heaven." (Matthew 5:20)

Background

This passage is from the sermon on the mountain, when Jesus shares his vision of what life is to be like with the coming of the reign of God. Jesus acknowledges the Law of Moses, yet he transcends it. The call of Jesus is much more challenging than the mere keeping of the Law. Rather, it is an invitation to a new way of being, to live more radically and authentically.

Reflection

Although we may not agree with what a fanatic stands for, we usually admire his or her commitment. Throughout the gospel, Jesus' invitation is for us to make nothing less than a wholehearted—and perhaps radical and certainly authentic—response to the love of God. This involves a willingness to grow and to be open to change—and change can be frightening. If we are afraid to change, we cannot expect to grow.

To Think About

At times it can be easier to remain a child.

Prayer

Lord, may I be willing to take responsibility for my life. Amen.

"Carry no money bag, no sack, no sandals; and greet no one along the way." (Luke 10:4)

October

15

Background

This verse gives us a sense of the urgency that accompanies the mission Jesus entrusts to his disciples. Even ordinary greetings should not be allowed to deter them in their single-mindedness. By the same token, they are not to get entangled in the things of this life. Jesus' disciples travel light without the clutter of material things.

Reflection

In our efforts to follow the gospel path, we can be handicapped and even sidetracked by our possessions or relationships. To discern whether something is a help or a hindrance, we have to be ruthlessly honest. If it's helpful, we should hang on to it and use it for the greater glory of God. If it is not helpful, it must be released or changed.

To Think About

"What can one give in exchange for his life?" (Matthew 16:26)

Prayer

Lord, you are my treasure. Amen.

October

16

"Whoever lives the truth comes to the light, so that his works may be clearly seen as done in God." *(John 3:21)*

Background

The expression "living the truth" predates the New Testament. It is found in the Old Testament and also in the rule of life for the community that lived at Qumran. The expression connotes "keeping faith" and implies that the one who does God's work comes to the light. The person who is set on doing God's work doesn't have anything to hide under the cover of darkness.

Reflection

Most people would agree with the saying: "The softest pillow is a clear conscience." In telling us that the truth will set us free (see John 8:32), Jesus is communicating a similar truth. When we live by the truth, we can live with ourselves knowing that apart from the Lord, the only person who really matters is the "person in the mirror"—ourselves! Shakespeare, like many another sage, reiterated this message when he encouraged us: "To thine own self be true."

To Think About

Why allow others to determine how I'm going to act?

Prayer

Lord, may a clear conscience be my daily reward. Amen.

"Everyone who acknowledges me before others . . . ." (Luke 12:8)

October

17

Background
The Greek verb for "acknowledge" is *homologeo*, which means "to proclaim aloud what God has accomplished." It implies that we should sing a magnificat, telling of how God has accomplished great things both within and through us. Members of the early Church know that this is important and necessary.

Reflection
William Elliott wrote: "To practical people, there is no oral or written evidence of the true religion so valid as the spectacle of its power to change bad men into good ones. Such a people will not accept arguments from history and from Scripture, but those of a moral kind they demand; they must see the theories at work." Christianity in action is the best possible witness to Christ.

To Think About
Example is the greatest of all seducers.
(French proverb)

Prayer
Lord, may I be a light in the darkness by living the gospel message. Amen.

October

18

"And should he come in the second or third watch and find them prepared in this way, blessed are those servants." (Luke 12:38)

Background

Whereas Jewish practice makes three watches, or divisions, of the night, the Romans divide the night into four. In Jesus' preaching, the disciples are frequently exhorted to be watchful, to be on their guard, because the enemy is forever on the prowl. What's more, watchfulness is considered to be one of the qualities of someone who is in love (see Song of Songs 5:2).

Reflection

A journey is much easier if we are well prepared for it. Instead of the customary last-minute rush, we find that our departure is smooth and relatively stress free if we have prepared carefully and thoroughly. We are able to leave on time, take our time, and remain on time. In the same way, if we live in a state of readiness to meet Jesus, we will be far more relaxed—able to enjoy life.

To Think About

I want to live every day as if it were my first day, my only day, and my last day.

Prayer

Lord, grant that I may be ready to meet you when you call. Amen.

"Much will be required of the person entrusted with much." (Luke 12:48)

Background
In this verse, found only in Luke's Gospel, Jesus is speaking about the leaders of the early Church who bear great responsibility. In the Old Testament we find that those who are chosen by God and given the help necessary for a special mission in life will suffer all the more if they fail to yield the expected fruit (see Amos 3:2; Hosea 4:4; Jeremiah 2:29).

Reflection
On the last day of lectures, the students were disappointed because the professor didn't give a clue as to what would appear on the final exam. One of the students remarked on how fortunate this actually was; because they were not told what was going to be on the test, the student reasoned, the standards would not be as high.

To Think About
Blessings come in various guises.

Prayer
Lord, may I live today as best I can and entrust yesterday and tomorrow to you. Amen.

October

19

"I have come to set the earth on fire." (Luke12:49)

Background

In Scripture, fire often indicates the presence of the Savior God. It is present in liturgical services where man meets his savior (see Leviticus 1:7ff), and it is also found where God reveals himself in what is termed a "theophany" (see Exodus 3:1ff; Ezekiel 1:4ff). It also has the meaning we find in this verse, whereby God comes with fire to judge and separate the good from the bad.

Reflection

When something is touched by fire it changes; normally it's destroyed. When Jesus touches the person, the "old person" is destroyed and a new one is born. This is the reason for Jesus' coming. Many of us, however, are frightened by the price involved in becoming totally Christ's. What we fail to realize is that before Jesus brings about any change within us, he first makes us want to change!

To Think About

Before he can use us, God may have to remake us.

Prayer

Lord, may I be totally yours. Amen.

"You know how to interpret the appearance of the earth and the sky...." (Luke 12:56)

Background
Jesus tells his listeners how people learn to understand and heed the signs they receive regarding the weather. In the same way, the immanence, or presence, of the kingdom of God can be seen in the various works and miracles Jesus performs. Unfortunately, these signs often go unheeded because of prejudice. People are not asked to be clever but to be open to the obvious.

Reflection
Like walking a tightrope, life necessitates keeping a balance between various conflicting values. Although we turn the other cheek, we are not expected to become a doormat for others. Although we need to be as shrewd as serpents, we must be as simple as doves. Jesus is ever ancient and yet ever new. We have to blend the new with the old and take care that we do not reject the new because of being entrenched within the old.

To Think About
If I fail to see Christ in the ordinary, I will not see him in the extraordinary.

Prayer
Lord, may I have the head of a sage and the heart of a child. Amen.

But he kept calling out all the more.
(Mark 10:48)

Background

Many great things fail to be accomplished because
people quit when they are at the point of success.
The blind Bartimaeus is a prime example of the
Latin adage: *perseverando vinces*—"Perseverance
wins!" As a cripple, Bartimaeus is one of the "little
ones" of the gospel. Because of his persistence, he
not only achieves his own healing, he becomes an
example of how we should pray.

Reflection

When asked by his teacher about the difference
between perseverance and obstinacy, little Johnny
replied: "Perseverance is a strong *will* and obstinacy
is a strong *won't.*" Whatever interpretation we
choose to give the word, perseverance enables us to
become the kind of person who is prepared to stick
to a task or a mission because it is essential for living a meaningful life.

To Think About

If a task is once begun, never leave it until it's
properly done.

Prayer

Lord, may I, like Bartimaeus, never give up. Amen.

"Which is easier, to say to the paralytic, 'Your sins are forgiven,' or to say, 'Rise, pick up your mat and walk'?" (Mark 2:9)

October

23

Background

For Jews, sin and sickness are inseparable. Persons are sick because they or one of their relatives has sinned. Jews also hold that only God can forgive sin, so for someone to claim this power is blasphemy, a crime punishable by stoning. To prove that he has the power to forgive sins, Jesus cures the sick man. Even this, however, is lost to the mind that is closed by prejudice.

Reflection

While being counseled in confession, a penitent was asked by the priest: "What would you do if you owned two houses?" "I would keep one and offer the other to someone who was homeless," the penitent replied. "And if you had two cars?" asked the priest. "I would keep one and give the other away," replied the penitent. "And if you had two horses?" asked the priest. "Oh!" replied the penitent, "I would keep them." "But why?" asked the priest. "Because I have two horses!" was the reply.

To Think About

To forgive another is to set myself free.

Prayer

Lord, enable me to forgive again and again and again. Amen.

October

24

"Sir, leave it for this year also, and I shall cultivate the ground around it. . . ." *(Luke 13:8)*

Background

At the time of Jesus it is not usual for a fig tree to be planted in a vineyard, because the soil, poor and shallow, will not support the tree's growth. Trees can only grow where the soil is rich and thick. Hence, the gardener's response! By cultivating the ground around the tree, there is some hope that fruit will eventually appear.

Reflection

A soldier was sentenced to death for deserting. When his mother pleaded with the general to have mercy on her son, the general replied: "But your son deserves no mercy." At this, the soldier's mother replied: "If he deserved mercy, then it wouldn't be mercy!" One of the beautiful aspects of mercy is that it is as hopeful as it is forgiving. As long as we believe that another can change, we will never lose hope.

To Think About

Others often have the knack of reflecting our weaknesses to us.

Prayer

Lord, may I always believe that you never create rubbish. Amen.

" . . . until the whole batch of dough was leavened." (Luke 13:21)

October

25

Background
In Jesus' time, of course, bread is baked at home. Leaven is a small piece of dough, kept from the last baking, that is allowed to ferment. Jesus has seen Mary put a piece of dough into the bread mixture, noticing that the whole character of the dough is changed because it is "leavened."

Reflection
It takes but a few moments to be baptized but a whole lifetime to become a Christian. Becoming a Christian has been compared to building a wall. Just as the wall is built brick by brick, so the Christian is "made" day by day. Each day is a gift given by God. We try to live for him and, eventually, he becomes part and parcel of the fabric of our every day. We, in turn, build a spiritual temple for him.

To Think About
Time has its own work to do. (P. Kavanagh)

Prayer
Lord, may my life reflect the time and love that you have invested in me. Amen.

October

26

"My mother and my brothers are those who hear the word of God and act on it." (Luke 8:21)

Background

In Matthew 10:36, we read that some of Jesus' kinsmen show up and try to constrain him because they genuinely think he is mad. For many, including some of his relatives, Jesus must be an embarrassment. For those who are on his wavelength, however, everything he says and does excites them and creates an inseparable bond among them.

Reflection

It has been said that the frightening aspect of a sin is experienced as such only the first time we commit the sin; eventually, we learn to accommodate the sin in our lives. While we may learn to live with sin, we know deep within that we are not at peace. Sin and peace are mutually exclusive. Only when we confront the sin in our lives can we begin to walk the road of peace.

To Think About

Every saint has a past; every sinner has a future. (Cardinal B. Hume)

Prayer

Guide me, Lord, in the path of your commands. Amen.

"Strive to enter through the narrow gate."
(Luke 13:24)

Background
The Greek word for "strive" is *agonizomai,* which implies strenuous muscular exercise and great physical effort. The English word "agony" is derived from the same word. Jesus is telling the Jews that being born a member of the chosen people is not sufficient for claiming membership of the kingdom of God. Rather, membership in the kingdom of God has to be worked for and demands a lifetime of effort—perhaps even agony.

Reflection
One reason people turn from the practice of religion is that they find it top-heavy with threats of hell and damnation. While all religion is intended to set us free, we must also realize that we can choose other than God. The choice is ours and it must be made many times each day. If we make a habit of choosing God in little things, we will have no problem when the big decisions come.

To Think About
Seek the Lord while he may be found. (Isaiah 55:6)

Prayer
Lord, keep me focused on what is important this day. Amen.

October

28

. . . he departed to the mountains to pray.
(Luke 6:12)

Background

Jesus is about to perform one of the most important tasks of his life; he is about to choose the twelve men—the apostles—who will carry his work forward long after he departs from them. Because it is a decision that will be vitally important for his messianic mission, Jesus prays. Time and again we find Jesus withdrawing to the solitude of nature to commune with the Father.

Reflection

Prayer necessitates leaving the place where we are. For Christians, prayer will often be the place where God's will is discovered, and this may necessitate our leaving behind old ways for something new. Going aside to pray requires that we leave what we have for something that God wants to give us. Only when we go before the Lord with an open agenda can our prayer be fruitful.

To Think About

Few people pray because few are prepared to accept the consequence of prayer.

Prayer

Lord, may I leave the tried and tested for the new and wonderful. Amen.

"Have you anything here to eat?" (Luke 24:41b)

Background
The risen body of Jesus is incapable of suffering and it has no need of food. Jesus, in an effort to convince the disciples of the reality of his resurrection, uses simple ordinary methods. For example, he invites his disciples to physically touch his wounds. Here we find him asking his disciples if they have anything to eat.

Reflection
So often we are confronted with our own poverty. This can come in many forms: the poverty of our emotions, financial poverty, the paucity of the skills that we possess, etc. However, there is a gift that each one of us can give: love in the form of caring. This can express itself in something as simple as a listening ear or through something as profound as an understanding heart.

To Think About
Some of the most important gifts I have to give—such as a smile—cost so little.

Prayer
Lord, may I trust that my poverty will be the gateway through which you will work. Amen.

October

30

"Master, we have worked hard all night and have caught nothing, but, at your command I will lower the nets." *(Luke 5:5)*

Background
Partly because of its tropical climate, the Sea of Galilee is noted for large shoals of fish that can cover the sea's floor as far as the eye can see. Although nighttime is considered to be the best time for fishing, Peter and his friends have fished all night with no success. Jesus, probably spotting the shoal of fish beneath the water's surface, asks Peter to let down the nets once again.

Reflection
It has been said that God created man in his own image and likeness and that man has kindly returned the compliment! Time and time again we reduce God to our limited standards. Because we fail to take him at his word, we fail to see his miracles at work in our lives. If only we would "do as he says," as Mary bids us (see John 2:5), we would find that our limited efforts are transformed beyond our greatest expectations.

To Think About
Can I afford to take Jesus at his word? Can I afford not to?

Prayer
Lord, may I live according to your word so that you might do your work through me. Amen.

"As for the seed that fell among thorns ... they are choked by the anxieties and riches and pleasures of life." (Luke 8:14)

October

31

Background
Some scholars hold that the parable of the sower depicts how the potential of the word of God depends on the heart into which it is sown. Others maintain that the aim of this parable is to provide encouragement against despair. Every farmer knows that some seed, inevitably, is going to be lost. This does not deter the farmer, however, from sowing the seed that will produce anything up to a hundredfold return.

Reflection
An old retired parish priest was visited by a former parishioner. The visitor was rather surprised to find that the priest had only a table, a chair, and some books. During their conversation, he asked the priest: "Where is your furniture?" "And where is yours?" asked the priest in reply. "Mine? But I'm only a visitor here," replied the former parishioner. "And so am I," replied the priest.

To Think About
The less I carry through life, the more quickly I can travel.

Prayer
Lord, may I learn to appreciate all that I have and to share with those less fortunate. Amen.

November

1

"Blessed are the peacemakers." (Matthew 5:9)

Background
It has been suggested that the word *shalom* means everything that helps foster humankind's highest good. In light of this understanding, we can translate this beatitude as: "Blessed are those who make this world a better place for people to live in." We pass this way but once and, hopefully, we will leave behind us a bouquet of beauty for God and others through the works we do.

Reflection
Frequently on our journey through life, we may win a battle but lose a war. All too often it takes a fatal illness, even a death, to make us realize how stupid we have been in harboring grievances. The road to peace begins with one small step. This can take the form of a phone call, a letter, or a simple greeting. If there is to be peace, it must begin with each one of us individually.

To Think About
In modern warfare there are no victors; there are only survivors. (L.B. Johnson)

Prayer
May *shalom* be your greeting of peace, O Lord, that I carry to the world. Amen.

. . . and gave them to the disciples, who in turn gave them to the crowds. (Matthew 15:36)

Background
The story of the feeding of the four thousand is generally seen as another version of the feeding of the five thousand, found in Matthew 14. One reason that both stories exist could be attributed to the fact that the story was often told within the early Church. This, in turn, would probably have linked it to the Eucharist, which it foreshadows in so many ways.

Reflection
Jesus never tries to "go it alone." Rather, he always attempts to make use of the gifts of those about him. This is one of the most beautiful blessings we can bestow on another, because people need to be needed. As we prepare for Christmas, it is important for us to open our eyes to Jesus who is already present in those about us. Unless we find him in our fellow pilgrims, it is doubtful we will find him on Christmas Day.

To Think About
There is nobody as poor as the person who doesn't need others.

Prayer
Lord, open my eyes to the giftedness of those about me. Amen.

November

3

"He [the older son] became angry, and . . . he refused to enter the house." *(Luke 15:28)*

Background

Most commentators see the older son as representing the self-righteous Pharisees who prefer to see a sinner destroyed rather than saved. So great is the resentment of the Pharisees, in fact, that they refuse to enter the kingdom that Jesus comes to establish. They are going to have no trucking with sinners such as the Gentile—or, in this story, the wayward son.

Reflection

In *The Prophet,* Kahlil Gibran writes: "Oftentimes have I heard you speak of one who commits a wrong as though he were not one of you, but a stranger unto you and an intruder upon your world. But I say that even as the holy and the righteous cannot rise beyond the highest which is in each one of you, so the wicked and the weak cannot fall lower than the lowest which is in you also." As our brothers and sisters are, so are we!

To Think About

"Let the one among you who is without sin be the first to throw a stone." (John 8:7)

Prayer

Father, I have sinned against heaven and against you. Amen.

... he sent [them] ahead of him in pairs ...
(Luke 10:1)

Background
The passage from which this verse is taken
describes a wider mission than the first mission to
which Jesus sends the Twelve. The apostolate is
expanding and, consequently, the numbers needing
to be trained are growing. While much can be
learned from the Master, it has to be applied in the
school of life, and the sending out is the formal initi-
ation of this group of disciples.

Reflection
Spiritual or soul friends are worth their weight in
gold. Often we are led to such spiritual guides after
prayer and searching. Ideally, they act as sounding
boards, reflecting back to us what they hear or
observe. They do not hesitate to call us to task if
they feel we have departed from the "straight and
narrow." Guided by their honest wisdom, we are able
to journey in the right direction on our quest.

To Think About
A friend is one who warns you. (Jewish proverb)

Prayer
Lord, may I love others enough to speak the truth in
love. Amen.

November

5

"The laborer deserves his payment." (Luke 10:7)

Background

Jesus has just commanded his disciples not to weigh themselves down with unnecessary baggage. The less they have, the freer they will be to devote themselves to the work of the kingdom. By the same token, they should be given the necessary support that will enable them to be free of any worry about providing for the basic necessities of life.

Reflection

Sometimes payment is made as if it were a charitable handout. Payment, however, has little to do with charity and everything to do with justice. Charity is giving to others that which is ours; justice is giving to others that which is already theirs. We have every right to ask for a just day's work in return for a just day's pay. By the same token, we have the duty to give a just day's work in return for a just day's pay!

To Think About

"How many people work in the Vatican, Holy Father?" "About half!"
(Attributed to Pope John XXIII)

Prayer

Lord, enable me to appreciate the fact that work can be an expression of love made visible. Amen.

"Nothing will be impossible for God." (Luke 1:37)

November

6

Background
The account of the Annunciation sets the stage for
the entry of Jesus who will herald the advent of a
new age and the beginning of a new kingdom. In
keeping with all the great heroes of history, and
because Jesus is special, his birth is heralded by an
angel. Being a virgin, Mary knows that she cannot
have conceived a child. This conception is done by
divine intervention, for nothing is impossible
for God.

Reflection
We so often determine how others act by what we
expect of them. Parents mold their children, in part,
by the way in which they expect their children to
behave. In a sense, we limit what God can do for us
by our lack of expectation. If nothing is impossible
to him, then the sky is the limit in what we should
ask of him. While he may not grant us our wants, he
will grant us all of our needs.

To Think About
Sometime during this day, I will fulfill one need that
another has by using one of my own gifts.

Prayer
Seek the face of the God of Jacob. (Psalm 24:6)

The hand of the Lord was with him. (Luke 1:66)

Background

More than thirty years pass after Jesus ascends into heaven before the first words of the New Testament are written. They are written, understandably, from the perspective of the resurrection and an early Church—a Church that has grown so rapidly that it has become a threat to the establishment. From this standpoint, we can appreciate how the author must have realized just how much the hand of God was with Jesus.

Reflection

How often we hear that all people are born equal— but some more equal than others! Within the Christian family, we are all born equals and there are no favorites. Through baptism we know that we are temples of the Holy Spirit, that God is living within us. Believing this, we know, too, that we can handle anything this day with God's help.

To Think About

I will contact a person who is in need of my love or forgiveness.

Prayer

You are God my Savior. (Psalm 25:5)

"... to give his people knowledge of salvation."
(Luke 1:77)

Background
These words of Zechariah refer to the unique mission that belongs to his son, John the Baptist. John is to be the one who prepares the way for the coming of the Son of God. This preparation involves a preaching of repentance and the forgiveness of sin. To John falls the task of awakening within the Jews, and within all those who will accept it, the expectation that their liberation is close at hand.

Reflection
We have been put on earth by God to fulfill some particular mission. The greatest thing we can ever hope to do is to bring others closer to the Lord by showing them the beauty that is within them. How can we expect others to know that they are loved by a God they have never seen unless they can experience God's love through those they can see?

To Think About
By acknowledging the beautiful aspects of the nature of others, perhaps I can help them pull back the veil that prevents them from seeing their own beauty.

Prayer
The promise of the Lord I will sing forever.
(Psalm 89:2)

November

9

"The Spirit of the Lord is upon me, because he has anointed me." (Luke 4:18)

Background

Quoting from Isaiah 61, Jesus angers the people in the synagogue with the way he speaks of the Gentiles. Convinced of their special position as a people that God has chosen, the Jews barely manage to tolerate the Gentiles, whom they hold in contempt. Yet, Jesus speaks of a special mission to all people regardless of their status.

Reflection

Like Jesus, we have been anointed and the Spirit of the Lord has come upon us. As with any gift, the Spirit is given for a purpose: to be shared with others. We are commissioned to bring good news to the poor, to proclaim liberty to those who are held captive by their fears, and to give new sight to those who may be blind to their own beauty and worth. Our mission is vast but our resources are adequate.

To Think About

So often the most difficult people to minister to are those of my own household.

Prayer

Lord, in the business of this day open my eyes to my real vocation. Amen.

". . . God has visited his people." (Luke 7:16b)

Background

Jesus is on a journey to Nain and, as he approaches the city, he is met by a funeral procession. A young man, "the only son of his mother," has died and his body is being brought for burial. We are then told that Jesus "was moved with pity" for the woman. This phrase summarizes the motif for the whole gospel: God takes pity on fallen humanity and sends his only Son to save us from our sin.

Reflection

Through the life that he lives, Jesus is able to authenticate the gospel he preaches. People will recognize the gospel when it is lived by another. For example, few people have attempted to justify the life that Mother Teresa lived; it spoke for itself. Illustrated Christianity never needs an explanation. Christ is the vine; we are the branches. It is through each one of us individually that Jesus will walk upon the face of the earth today—but only if we allow him to!

To Think About

Who does God wish to visit this day by means of me?

Prayer

Lord, I'm yours, especially for today. Amen.

November

11

"To what shall I compare the people of this generation?" (Luke 7:31)

Background
The Pharisees are constantly thwarting God's purpose in order to achieve their own selfish ends. What should be their moment of triumph, the coming of the Messiah, is to become their moment of doom. Here we find Jesus, utterly frustrated and at the end of his patience, lamenting their closed minds and hearts that result in their intransigence.

Reflection
There's a lot of wisdom in the old adage that says there are none so deaf as those who do not wish to hear. However, if we are alive to the gospel, we will want to hear the voice of God as he calls to us through the various episodes of our lives. If we are faithful in heeding what the gospel asks of us, we are promised a richness of life that this world cannot give.

To Think About
Can I afford five minutes today to rest with a gospel passage?

Prayer
Lord, may the doing of your will be the only purpose that I need today. Amen.

"Blessed are you when people hate you . . . on account of the Son of Man." (Luke 6:22)

Background
This beatitude is particularly applicable to the early Church, which experiences persecution well into the fourth century. Jesus is ruthlessly honest with his disciples. He does not promise them an easy life; rather, he promises them a quality of life that is beyond anything this world can offer.

Reflection
During the persecutions, groups of Christians would gather secretly to pray, knowing that being caught would mean imprisonment and even death. During one such gathering, the door was kicked open and a soldier brandishing a weapon said: "Any Christians here have one minute to get out." As the soldier made ready to act on his threat, a few in the gathered group moved cautiously to the door and dashed off. When it was apparent that nobody else was going to leave, the soldier closed the door, put down his weapon, and said: "I, too, am Christian and we're better off without that lot!"

To Think About
When did I last have to suffer for being a Christian?

Prayer
Lord, may I value you above all other riches. Amen.

November

13

"For behold, the kingdom of God is among you."
(Luke 17:21)

Background
This saying of Jesus relates to questions about the Christian observance of the Mosaic Law. According to Luke, the presence of Jesus and the reign of the Holy Spirit are the initial stages of the kingdom that will achieve its fullness in a future age. It has little to do with a heartless observance of the Law.

Reflection
As Christians, we are called to establish the kingdom of God here on earth, that is, we are called to bring heaven down to earth. To want only what God wants, both for ourselves and others, is the essence of the kingdom of God. We reveal the kingdom, as the Second Vatican Council tells us, by being Christ's word to others, doing his work, and being his presence.

To Think About
The kingdom of God is a kingdom of love; and love is never a stagnant pool. (H. W. Du Bose)

Prayer
Thy kingdom come, thy will be done by me and through me. Amen.

"I am not worthy to have you enter my roof."
(Luke 7:6)

Background
The centurion has the equivalent rank of a regimental sergeant-major and, as such, is one of the high-ranking officers of the Roman army. He knows that Jesus will become legally "unclean" if he enters his house because he is a non-Jew—a Gentile. For the same reason, Jews are forbidden to allow Gentiles into their homes or to have any dealings with them whatsoever.

Reflection
There are as many pathways to God as there are individuals. One of the most beautiful qualities that a Christian can have is toleration of the customs of another. While we may neither understand nor agree with others, we must always respect them as human beings created by God. Where tolerance and consideration prevail, love will flourish—and where love flourishes, God is present.

To Think About
I do to others as I would want them to do to me.

Prayer
Lord, may I value my way of life while realizing that there are other ways of living. Amen.

November

15

"So by their fruits you will know them."
(Matthew 7:20)

Background

Greeks, Romans, and Jews hold that a tree is to be classed by the fruit it produces. The Jewish teachers—the rabbis—are obliged to have a trade that earns them a living. They are never allowed to take payment for their teaching. Many rabbis, however, are motivated by what they can get out of teaching rather than what they might give to others.

Reflection

Almost all of the fruits produced about us are unnoticed. Occasionally we may advert to a piece of fruit when we happen to eat it. It is the same with the lives of others. While noting the mistakes of others, we often miss the good that they perform. Before we dare to judge it is necessary for us to see the complete picture—which is known to God alone!

To Think About

Many an act is destined to go unnoticed by all except God.

Prayer

May I see first the good in others, O Lord, not their mistakes. Amen.

"Are you the one who is to come, or should we look for another?" (Luke 7:19)

November

16

Background

The "one who is to come," a technical term taken from Malachi 3:1, 23, refers to a person who is expected in Palestinian Judaism and who will be associated with the Messiah. Because Jesus fails to clearly identify himself, and because he is slow in establishing his kingdom, John the Baptist begins to have his doubts. He sends his disciples to Jesus with this question.

Reflection

Christians are called to make Christ present, to be "other Christs." They do this primarily through the actions of their own lives and in the way they treat others. Regardless of our past, it is today that we are called upon to incarnate the gospel. As we begin the rest of our lives, we are invited to commit all that we do to Jesus. It is never too late to start, and nobody is ever too insignificant to be used by God.

To Think About

For a web begun, God sends thread.
(Italian proverb)

Prayer

Lord, I'm yours for the using. Amen.

November

17

"I do not seek my own will but the will of the one who sent me." *(John 5:30)*

Background
In this passage, Jesus is setting out his teaching about judgment, and he justifies his right to judge. This right, he claims, comes from being so at one with the Father's wishes that he knows perfectly well what the mind of God is. Jesus claims that the Father and he are united in such a way that, in fact, they are one (see John 10:30).

Reflection
The underlying desire within every human being is to be happy, and the surest way to achieve this happiness is by doing what God asks. While doing God's will is certain to bring happiness, there is no guarantee that it will bring great fame or wealth—these are not substitutes for happiness! Ninety-nine percent of the time, what we will and what God wills are the same. The other one percent of the time, our conscience will tell us that there's a problem. The choice, then, will determine our eventual happiness.

To Think About
Is my prayer, "Lord, do this"?

Prayer
Lead, kindly light, lead thou me on. Amen.

"Woe to you, scribes and Pharisees, you ... have neglected the weightier things of the law: judgment and mercy and fidelity." (Matthew 23:23)

Background

Determining what forms of produce come under the law of tithing is the problem here. Those who adhere to the exact minutiae, claim that all natural growth is subject to the Law. The more realistic interpretation, however, limits the obligation to the traditional grain, wine, and oil. Tiny seeds, such as mint, dill, and cumin, are so small that it would be ridiculous to tithe them.

Reflection

We're told that it's bad to allow our hearts to rule our heads. But could we not argue that the opposite can be equally true! If religious people were to follow the instinct of their hearts rather than the logic of their religion, our world would be spared a lot of suffering. People often become cruel when they succumb to an ideology. Compassion has no ideology.

To Think About

Pagans are people who do not need to quarrel about religion!

Prayer

Lord, that I may see. Amen.

"... He has sent me to proclaim liberty to captives ..." (Luke 4:18)

Background

Jesus comes to the synagogue in his hometown to set out his plan. He does this by reading from the opening verses of Isaiah 61. The particular form of the verb "sent" implies more than just being sent on a mission. Rather, it signifies that the one being sent is already present. This is what Jesus is trying to communicate to his listeners. Unlike the preaching of John, which emphasizes the wrath of God, Jesus is proclaiming good news that is both healing and liberating.

Reflection

Fear imprisons most of us. We get to a point where we find it difficult to distinguish between the really imagined and the imagined real. Illusion and imagination consort together to rob us of our peace. It is said that there is nothing to fear but fear itself. Jesus is the one who wants to liberate those of us who are held captive by our various fears. To us he says, "Do not be afraid."

To Think About

The past and the future can rob us of our liberty; the great opportunity is the present.

Prayer

Thank you, Father, that you are always with me. Amen.

"For this reason a man shall leave his father and mother [and be joined to his wife] and the two shall become one flesh." (Mark 10:7-8)

Background
Genesis 2:23 tells us that woman is taken from man and is "bone of my bones and flesh of my flesh," and this is why a man's unity with his wife becomes stronger than the bond he might have with his closest blood relatives. Jesus speaks against the loose sexual morality of his day and makes a fortress of the home and the family.

Reflection
A woman was attending a lecture when suddenly she jumped up and left the hall. Fearing that the woman was ill, another woman followed her and found her making a phone call. "Is everything O.K?" she asked, to which the woman on the phone responded. "Oh, yes. You see, today is bin day and I cannot lift them to put them out, whereas my husband can't remember to do it." Success, even in marriage, demands teamwork.

To Think About
Success demands teamwork.

Prayer
Lord, may I spend my life for others. Amen.

November

21

"...and God is glorified in him." *(John 13:31)*

Background
The greatest expression of the glory of God lies in the Incarnation and the cross. These are the two means by which God's love for the world is expressed most clearly. Because they represent an expression of infinite love, they evoke a loving response. It is through coming among us and eventually giving his life for us that Jesus gives the greatest glory to the Father.

Reflection
When Johann Sebastian Bach died in 1750, there were very few who knew of his genius in musical composition. It was Felix Mendelssohn who, through his discovery and performance of Bach's "St. Matthew Passion," showed him to the world as the genius he was. On the side of Bach's manuscript, as on many others, were the words: "To God Alone the Glory." If we work for the glory of God, we can only succeed.

To Think About
Provided God be glorified, we must not care by whom. (Saint Francis de Sales)

Prayer
To you alone, O Lord, be all the glory. Amen.

"I was sent to speak to you and to announce to you this good news." (Luke 1:19)

November

22

Background
The passage from which this verse is taken deals with the announcement of the conception and birth of John the Baptist, the precursor of Jesus. It is the archangel Gabriel who, in the Old Testament, announces to the prophet Daniel the time when the Messiah would come (see Daniel 8:15-26). It is the same archangel Gabriel who will announce to Mary the events connected with the Incarnation of Jesus.

Reflection
In our baptism we are called to be missionaries. We are called to proclaim the gospel by both word and example, wherever we my find ourselves. All too often we shy away from this, professing that we're not competent enough or sufficiently eloquent. God has put us in the place where he wants us to be, however, and has given us all the talents we need. He has entrusted to each of us individually a mission that nobody else can accomplish.

To Think About
God can write straight, even when the lines appear crooked!

Prayer
Lord, sing your song through me this day. Amen.

November

23

They all ate and were satisfied. (Luke 9:17a)

Background
Whenever Jesus sets out to do anything, he never does it by halves. Whether it is satisfying the thirst of the woman at the well or the hunger of the five thousand, Jesus always gives people more than enough.

Reflection
It takes relatively little to satisfy our basic needs. However, like the ripples that flow from a pebble dropped into a pool, our basic needs appear to become larger as we grow from childhood to adulthood. Quite often our contentment decreases accordingly. Yet, the secret of contentment lies not so much in acquiring more but in developing the ability to enjoy less.

To Think About
Contentment is being satisfied with what I have, rather than getting what I want.

Prayer
Lord, make me truly grateful for all that I now possess. Amen.

Then the fever left her and she waited on them.
(Mark 1:31)

November
24

Background
The Talmud mentions "a burning fever" that is quite common in Galilee. When Jesus arrives at the house of Peter's mother-in-law, he is told of her situation and he does the most caring thing he could do: He cures her. No sooner is she cured than she begins to attend to the needs of others. She uses her gift of recovered health to be of service to others.

Reflection
As soon as she is given the gift of good health, Peter's mother-in-law uses this gift to serve Jesus and his companions. Likewise, the gifts we are given are meant for the service of God and others. A smile, a word of encouragement, a helping hand, may be the greatest gifts we have to use this day. By means of these gifts, the lives of others will be enriched and, in the process, we will find we have become happier people.

To Think About
Unselfish service is the rent we pay for a life of happiness.

Prayer
Lord, give me a contagious smile today. Amen.

November

25

"How can you say to your brother, 'Let me remove that splinter from your eye,' while the wooden beam is in your eye?" (Matthew 7:4)

Background

Within each one of us there is a secret room where we store things that we don't want others to know are part of our character. When we reflect on these secret things, they can have a sobering effect on us. Have you ever noticed how, when you point a finger at another, you always find that you are pointing three at yourself. Indeed, people in glass houses should never throw stones.

Reflection

For the Jew, leniency in judging one's neighbor was a sacred duty, along with devotion to prayer, educating the young in the Law, visiting the sick, hospitality, and study. It was one of the six great ways in which a person could win favor, both in this world and in the world to come. In short, we are advised that judging another is beyond our mandate; it belongs to God alone.

To Think About

I will be careful about the bridges I burn; I may yet need to cross them.

Prayer

Lord, help me to get my own house in order before I dare touch another's. Amen.

"Sir, we would like to see Jesus." (John 12:21b)

Background
Some non-Jews have come to Jerusalem as pilgrims or sightseers. One can only speculate as to why they might have desired to see Jesus, but their desire highlights the dismissal of Jesus by the Jewish leaders, who should have been the first ones to accept him. It is interesting that the Gentiles' request is made through Andrew and Philip, the only two of the apostles who bear Greek names.

Reflection
The children were shouting and making a bit of a commotion in the next room. When she couldn't tolerate it any longer, the children's mother stormed into the room and demanded to know what they were quarrelling about. "Oh, we're not quarrelling," answered the eldest. "We're just playing Mommy and Daddy." Example teaches in ways that words can never hope to.

To Think About
Few things are harder to put up with than the annoyance of good example. (M. Twain)

Prayer
May your love radiate within my life. Amen.

November

27

"Anyone who gives you a cup of water to drink
because you belong to Christ . . . will surely not
lose his reward." (Mark 9:41)

Background

Hospitality is a priority for the Jews. Jesus reminds
his listeners that anything they do or give to
another, no matter how small it is, will not go
unrewarded. Jesus explains that the person who
happens to be in need belongs to him, that what we
give is not important, and that the simple things are
as important as the more difficult.

Reflection

"See how these Christians love one another" is the
remark made by pagans when they see the early
Christians interacting with one another. It was not
theology, status, or power that set them apart from
others but their mutual love. It has been said that we
get to heaven on the back of one another, so I wonder which fellow Christian is depending on me for a
helping hand this day?

To Think About

If we love one another, God remains in us.
(1 John 4:12)

Prayer

Lord, while I will love those I like, may you, working
in me, love those I dislike. Amen.

"Follow me." (Matthew 8:22)

November

28

Background
The phrase "following Jesus" has a precise meaning. A follower of Jesus is one who is called to believe his doctrine, imbibe his Spirit, and imitate his example; in short "following Jesus' means being Jesus' disciple. It necessitates making oneself totally available to Jesus, regardless of the sacrifices or depravation this might entail.

Reflection
When Jesus asks anything of his disciples in the Gospels, there is little ambiguity about his request. Just as he calls some to be his disciples two thousand years ago, he calls us today, and his invitation is a straightforward "follow me." We have to hear this call—and respond to it—within the details of our own lives. Simply put, following Jesus is a call to live the gospel message today.

To Think About
. . . live in a manner worthy of the call you have received. (Ephesians 4:1)

Prayer
Lord, enable me to hear your call so that I may faithfully follow. Amen.

November

29

"Go home to your family and announce to them all that the Lord in his pity has done for you." (Mark 5:19)

Background

This meeting between Jesus and the man who had been possessed takes place in the Decapolis, which means "The Ten Cities"—cities that, although they are Greek, they are subject to Roman taxation. This is the first recorded contact that Jesus has with this civilization and it is to have enormous consequences. The man who had been possessed is chosen to be a witness for Christ among his own people.

Reflection

Quite often we find that it is easier to share at a deep level with an "outsider" than with a family member. One of the reasons for this is that familiarity often breeds contempt. However, it is within the family that our values are formed and scrutinized. By sharing our struggles with those at home, we can find ourselves loved more deeply while being instrumental in molding our loved ones in the likeness of Christ.

To Think About

What a father says to his children is not heard by the world, but it will be heard by posterity. (J. P. Eixhter)

Prayer

Lord, may I have the strength to share what is deepest with those who are closest. Amen.

"Beware that your hearts do not become drowsy from . . . the anxieties of daily life." (Luke 21:34)

Background

This gospel passage has two key elements. It begins with an account of the second coming of Jesus and ends with Luke's exhortation to be awake and vigilant. Only in this section of the Gospels is the Greek word for redemption (*apolytrosis*) to be found. It literally means "to repurchase," and it has a similar underlying meaning to the Old Testament idea of redemption.

Reflection

When the poet W. H. Davies wrote, "What is this life if full of care, we have no time to stand and stare," he had his finger on the pulse of modern-day living. Despite our modern time-saving devices, we seem to have less free time than ever. As nature winds down for a time of quiet hibernation in the approach of winter, we are invited to use this season of Advent to see where we are going—or perhaps to see where we are not going—on our journey of life.

To Think About

The unexamined life is not worth living. (Socrates)

Prayer

Lord, teach me your ways so that I may walk in your paths. Amen.

December

1

" . . . only say the word and my servant will be healed." (Matthew 8:8)

Background

The spotlight in this passage is not so much on the healing that Jesus accomplishes but on the faith and kindness of the centurion. In Luke's account of this same incident, the "servant" is called *dulos*, or slave. The centurion's attitude to the servant/slave is striking, because within the Roman Empire a slave is worthless. Aristotle states: "A master and slave have nothing in common." This centurion's attitude is, indeed, exceptional.

Reflection

One of the many lessons that the Gospels teach us is the power of the divine over the human. As we read the Gospels, we notice how Jesus has the power to calm storms and heal those who are deemed incurable; in short, Jesus turns the impossible into the possible. If we trust him, he can do the same for us. The only thing that often limits his power is the limitation that is caused by our lack of faith in him.

To Think About

I have the strength for everything through him who empowers me. (Philippians 4:13)

Prayer

Lord, come within me so that you may come to others through me. Amen.

"Blessed are the eyes that see what you see."
(Luke 10:23)

December

2

Background
This single beatitude comes within a short passage where Jesus is telling his disciples how privileged they are. While prophets and kings lived in the hope of seeing the day when the Messiah would come, the disciples are actually the ones who experience the event. In the person of Jesus, they are witnessing how all of history is reaching its fulfillment.

Reflection
We are told that faraway hills always look greener and that others often seem to have been dealt a better hand in life than we've been dealt. What we fail to appreciate is that we have been given all the ingredients we need to experience happiness and live life to the full. Until we realize just how blessed we are, we will find ourselves being envious of others. The measure of our happiness depends on how grateful we are.

To Think About
Things could be better—but then again, they could be a mighty lot worse!

Prayer
Lord, may I realize just how much I'm spoiled by you. Amen.

December

3

"My heart is moved with pity for the crowd."
(Matthew 15:32)

Background

Throughout the Gospels, compassion is one of the great motivating factors for Jesus. Compassion causes Jesus to reach out and meet the needs of the whole person. He is concerned to provide healing not just for the soul but also for the body. Here we find Jesus concerned about those people who have been following him and who are hungry.

Reflection

Sympathy is the haven that often enables another to weather life's storms. Each one of us has experienced the therapeutic effect of a listening ear—not to mention a listening heart. One Indian language translates the word friend as "one who carries my sorrows on his back." How better to prepare for the coming of Christ than by welcoming him in the brothers and sisters we encounter on our journey to Christmas.

To Think About

People don't really care about how much I know; they are far more concerned about how much I care.

Prayer

Lord, transform my heart of stone into a heart of love. Amen.

"Not everyone who says to me, 'Lord, Lord,' will enter the kingdom of heaven." (Matthew 7:21)

December

4

Background
The title "Lord" is used extensively by the primitive Church. Jesus is telling his followers that it is not enough just to preach about the kingdom in order to enter it. Rather, one has to practice what one preaches. Jesus always equates discipleship and love of him with doing the will of his Father. Ultimately, it is our actions that speak far louder than our words!

Reflection
Few of us need to be told that actions speak louder than words. Jesus is at pains to teach that entry into the kingdom of heaven is by means of actions and not by birthright or what one preaches. Even when he foretells what the last judgment will comprise, the questions that will be asked of us will focus on what we have done: "I was hungry and what did you do about it? I was thirsty and what did you do about it?"

To Think About
A loaf of bread is better than a million words to a hungry person.

Prayer
Lord, help me to solve this world's problems by what I do rather than by the words I speak. Amen.

December

5

But they went out and spread word of him through all that land. (Matthew 9:31)

Background

Jesus does not want his role as Messiah to be proclaimed too soon because he first wants his audience to realize the kind of Messiah he is. Thus when the two blind men come to Jesus for help and their sight is restored, they are asked to keep the matter quiet. We are told, however, that they don't. Saint Jerome tells us that the reason these two blind men tell everyone about their restored sight is that this is their only way of expressing their gratitude.

Reflection

When we encounter Christ, we cannot help telling others about him. It is as if, through us, he becomes contagious. Others notice that something has happened within us and they envy us, wishing that they could have a similar life-giving experience. Unless we encounter Christ through one another, Christmas will come and go, leaving us with little more than a lighter wallet and a larger waistline.

To Think About

What image of Christ do I present to others by my lifestyle?

Prayer

Lord, may your Bethlehem be within me this Christmas. Amen.

"The harvest is abundant but the laborers are few." (Matthew 9:37)

Background
While the Pharisees of the time look at the great mass of people with a disdain bordering on contempt, Jesus sees in these same people a rich harvest waiting to be reaped. Knowing that he is going to entrust the continuation of his work to his disciples, Jesus speaks of their missionary work as a harvest that is waiting to be reaped (see John 4:35ff).

Reflection
There is some truth in the saying that "too many cooks spoil the broth." Sometimes, it seems that more work gets accomplished when there are less helpers. It's as if the few who gather to help become more committed to the task at hand. If we decide to join the laborers, we will be called to give our utmost commitment. There will be no abundance and little pay—but the promise of a great pension!

To Think About
A big effort from a few people is often better than a half-hearted effort from many.

Prayer
Lord, may I learn to give without counting the cost. Amen.

December

6

December

7

"*Prepare the way of the Lord, make straight his paths.*" *(Luke 3:4)*

Background

This quotation comes from Isaiah 40:3-5. At that time, when a king proposed to pay a visit to any part of his domain, messengers were sent well in advance so that the people could repair the roads for the king's travels. In this context, John the Baptist is the messenger who is sent ahead of Jesus to prepare the minds and hearts of the people for Jesus' coming.

Reflection

When artist William Holman Hurt finished painting "Jesus Knocking at the Door," a friend of his pointed out that he had forgotten to put a latch on the out-side of the door. In reply Hunt said: "No! It resembles the human heart which can only be opened from within." For Christmas to be a reality, there may be some thing or some relationship that needs to change, but this will have to happen from within the heart. Jesus will not enter unbidden.

To Think About

To make room for Jesus within the crib of my heart, something may need to go.

Prayer

Deliver me, Lord, from my bondage. Amen.

"May it be done to me according to your word."
(Luke 1:38)

December

8

Background
Mary struggles to understand what is being asked of her. Her initial experience of fear is replaced by her effort to comprehend just how this could happen. Finally, the scene reaches a beautiful crescendo when we encounter Mary wanting only what God is asking of her and nothing more.

Reflection
When we come to know God as Father, we learn to trust in a new way. We also learn that God knows what is best for us and will never allow anything to happen to us that is not for our good. We have to learn to entrust our lives completely to God, our Father. When we do this, we are able to make our own the prayer of Mary: "May it be done to me according to your word" (Luke 1:38).

To Think About
What would happen to my life if I were to entrust it completely to God, my Father?

Prayer
Be it done unto me today, Lord, according to your word. Amen.

December

9

"If a man has a hundred sheep and one of them goes astray, will he not leave the ninety-nine in the hills and go in search of the stray?" *(Matthew 18:12)*

Background
Sheep, by nature, are gregarious animals and so normally stay together. At the time of Jesus, flocks are often grazed together, with perhaps as few as two or three shepherds tending a particular flock. Normally, if a sheep goes astray, the shepherd has to search for it and bring back the sheep or its fleece (as proof that the sheep was dead).

Reflection
Life has been described as a game of hide-and-seek, whereby God comes in search of us when we stray from his ways. Until we come to appreciate the extent to which God is prepared to go in order to woo us back to him, we can never hope to understand how inestimably valuable we are in his sight. He loves us so much that he even gives us his only Son—the greatest Christmas gift we will ever receive.

To Think About
Only when I come to realize that I am a sinner will I feel the need of a Savior.

Prayer
Lord, save me from the consequences of my willful ways. Amen.

"For my yoke is easy, and my burden light."
(Matthew 11:30)

10

Background
Saint Augustine compared the weight of Christ's
yoke to the weight of the wings of a bird. In Sermon
126, he said: "If you take a bird's wings away, you
might seem to be taking weight off it, but the more
weight you take off, the more you tie it down to the
earth … Give it back the weight of its wings and you
will see how it flies."

Reflection
Before he became Pope John Paul I, Cardinal Albino
Luciani went into a religious shop to buy a small
crucifix. The shopkeeper apologized and explained
that he had none in stock. He then went on to offer
some crosses that were similar in size and price. The
cardinal thanked the shopkeeper but declined his
offer saying: "A cross without Jesus would be too
heavy to carry." In any situation, Jesus and I are
sufficient!

To Think About
If God is for us, who can be against us?
(Romans 8:31)

Prayer
Lord, make haste to help me. Amen.

December

11

"The kingdom of heaven suffers violence, and the violent are taking it by force." (Matthew 11:12)

Background

This verse is obscure in both Matthew and Luke (see Luke 16:16). One possible meaning is that the kingdom is under attack by those who are violent. It may also mean that the kingdom will be open to attack by its enemies, and those who wish to enter it must match the violence of its enemies with their own dedicated commitment. Still another interpretation is to see this verse against the backdrop of the Zealots, those contemporaries of Jesus who seek to establish the kingdom by violent means.

Reflection

To live within the kingdom is to allow every facet of our lives to be influenced by the demands of the gospel. This may demand that we make some difficult changes. God will not force these changes on us, however. Rather, he will help us make them. The peace that is central to Christmas is one of the rewards we will enjoy if we decide to pay the price. However, it may be that we feel the price is too high!

To Think About

What gift would I like to give myself this Christmas?

Prayer

Lord, may your kingdom come within me this Christmas. Amen.

"Do not be afraid, Mary, for you have found favor with God." (Luke 1:30)

December

12

Background
This greeting is similar to the one given a few verses earlier (see v. 28), where the angel attempts to put Mary at ease and allay her fears. It sets the stage for the drama that is about to unfold, where Mary is called to the greatest vocation ever offered to a human being: to be the mother of Jesus, the Mother of God.

Reflection
So often we act as if our salvation is something we can earn, failing to realize that it is a gift that has been won for us by Jesus. Left to ourselves, we are completely helpless. Like Mary, however, we have found favor with God. We are the ones in whom the Father is well pleased, so there is no need for fear. Advent is a reminder that God so loves the world— each of us individually—that he sends his only Son.

To Think About
Love removes fear.

Prayer
Lord, show me the Father's love. Amen.

"…*and they did not recognize him.*"
(Matthew 17:12)

Background

Among the Jews there is the growing belief that
Elijah will come to set all things in order before the
Messiah arrives. His visitation will be powerful, and
force will be used to put things in proper order.
Jesus is informing the Jews that he is the expected
Elijah, but they are unable to recognize him as such.

Reflection

How often we use the phrase: "If only I had known!"
Yet, many times each day we encounter Christ and
fail to recognize him, perhaps because we live in the
fast lane or because we fail to equate Jesus with our
brother or sister in need. Unless we learn to recognize the guises that he comes in during these days of
Advent, it's unlikely that we will recognize Jesus
when he comes on Christmas Day.

To Think About

I will take off my shoes because the ground on
which I walk is sacred.

Prayer

Lord, may I find you within me so that I may learn
to find you about me. Amen.

"Whoever has two cloaks should share with the person who has none." (Luke 3:11)

December

14

Background
One of the overriding features of John the Baptist's preaching is that it has a strong social justice message. Those who seek forgiveness must first be prepared to share their abundance with the neighbor who has less. This is to be one of the outstanding traits of Jesus' teaching, as found, for example, in the story of Dives and Lazarus (see Luke 16:19ff).

Reflection
When the people ask John what they need to do by way of preparation, his answer is scandalously materialistic: share your cloak, share your food! This is the invitation and the challenge made to each of us as we prepare for Jesus' coming. We are invited to shed some of our possessions so that Jesus will have a little bit more room within our lives.

To Think About
I have a gift that only I can use.

Prayer
Lord, may I make do with less in order to be open to receive more. Amen.

December

15

"We do not know." *(Matthew 21:27)*

Background

This scene is perhaps one of the most skillfully crafted pieces of Jesus' oratory recorded in the Gospels. It is the duty of the Sanhedrin to distinguish between true and false prophets. Yet, here we find them making a public confession that they are unable to do this. It is not so much that they do not know the answer but rather, they are unwilling to tell what they know to be the truth.

Reflection

As children, a couple of friends and I fancied ourselves as mini-philosophers. We were told that God could do everything and the question that often came up for debate was: "Could God actually lift a bald man up to heaven by the hair of his head?" So often we look to God not so much as a loving Father but as a magician. If we are prepared to do our bit, God will certainly meet us halfway.

To Think About

Those who don't want to see are the blindest of all.

Prayer

Lord, may I learn to accept you on your terms rather than on mine. Amen.

"Tax collectors and prostitutes are entering the kingdom of God before you." (Matthew 21:31)

Background

Jesus does not tolerate hypocrisy and leaves us in no doubt as to what he thinks of the Jewish leaders who are hypocritical in many ways. The tax collectors and prostitutes are two of the most despised classes in Jesus' day. By saying they will be entering the kingdom before their leaders, Jesus is informing the Jewish leaders that they are beneath the lowest social class.

Reflection

We have often heard it said that God has no favorites. In fact, if there is any group that he does show favor toward, it is those who are on the margins of society. There is always the danger that we might become complacent before God, even to the point of thinking we have some birthright to be treated above our fellow pilgrims. At best, we are unworthy servants.

To Think About

"Whatever you did for one of these least brothers of mine, you did for me." (Matthew.25:40)

Prayer

Lord, may my life be a sacrifice of gratitude to you. Amen.

... Jesus Christ, the son of David, the son of Abraham. (Matthew 1:1)

Background

Matthew's Gospel was written with the Jewish people in mind. It was important that Jesus' genealogy be well grounded in Jewish ancestry. Consequently, Matthew traces Jesus' genealogy through David— who was the finest king that the Jews had—right back to Abraham, the father of the Jews. In every sense, Jesus was Jewish through and through.

Reflection

One of our greatest needs as human beings is security. Sociologists tell us that with the breakdown of the family unit and especially the extended family, people are aware of their lack of roots, of not belonging, and thus they experience insecurity. If we are convinced that we are children of a loving Father, however, it will color all of our attitudes to life and others.

To Think About

I am created in the image and likeness of God.

Prayer

How majestic are your works, Lord, our God. Amen.

"... and they shall name him Emmanuel, which means 'God is with us.'" (Matthew 1:23)

December

18

Background

Matthew is alluding to the seven-hundred-year-old prophecy of Isaiah that foretold of the coming of the Messiah. That prophesy said that the Messiah's coming would be foretold by an extraordinary event, such as a virgin giving birth to a son. Jesus' coming initiates the messianic age, and Jesus inaugurates the presence of God among his people in an entirely new way.

Reflection

If we are honest, do we really think we need a savior? If we find ourselves in a situation where we're doing fine, this Christmas event will probably come and go without having much of an effect on us. When we realize our need for God we come to appreciate the gift of Christmas as never before. Simply put, Christmas becomes that point where our failures are embraced by the kiss of God.

To Think About

Mary has given humanity the greatest gift we have ever received.

Prayer

Come, Lord Jesus, come. Amen.

"Do not be afraid, Zechariah, because your prayer has been heard." (Luke 1:13)

Background

The phrase "Do not be afraid" often forms the pre-amble to a significant act of God. Here it is used to assure Zechariah that both he and Elizabeth will be blessed with the gift of a son who will be called John, a name that means "God is gracious." This child will be the one to prepare the way for the long-awaited Messiah.

Reflection

A young boy prayed that when he awoke, God would have answered his prayer for a big bunch of his favorite fruit: bananas! When morning came, how-ever, he was somewhat disappointed to find that there were no bananas. He felt that God had not listened. Almost twenty years later, he received his first paycheck and had enough money to buy all the bananas in town.

To Think About

Prayers are always answered in God's way and in God's time.

Prayer

Lord, may thy will be done. Amen.

But she was greatly troubled at what was said
and pondered what sort of greeting this might be.
(Luke 1:29)

December

20

Background
The Greek word for "pondering" is *dielogizeto*, which implies a period of prolonged and intense reflection. So often we are inclined to think that Mary had it all mapped out for her, but nothing could be further from the truth. When we reflect on the implications of the archangel's message, Mary actually had every reason to be troubled!

Reflection
A story is told of a young girl who came home one day with her report card. Underneath the heading "Spelling" there appeared the grade "F." When her mother asked why, the young girl replied: "Mother, I just don't know; words fail me!" We are in a similar situation with the mystery of the Incarnation; we will never fully understand the "why" of it. However, we are not asked to understand it but to accept it as gift.

To Think About
God loved me so much that he gave me his Son.

Prayer
Come, Lord Jesus, and quiet my troubled heart. Amen.

December

21

"Blessed are you who believed that what was spoken to you by the Lord would be fulfilled."
(Luke1:45)

Background
In this chapter, we find Mary's faith standing in stark contrast with that of Zechariah, who doubts God's promise. Luke suggests that Mary is blessed more because of the faith and obedience she shows than because of her privileged position as the one chosen to be the Mother of God. She is portrayed as the model of the attitude that a person of faith should have—complete submission to God's will.

Reflection
The entire story of God's dealing with humans is one of infidelity on the part of humans being surpassed by divine fidelity. We may well have promised to do or avoid doing something as a means of preparing for Jesus' coming at Christmas. Whether we have succeeded or failed is not important, however. Christmas will happen. A Savior will come because God has promised and he has yet to break a promise.

To Think About
It's never too late to do something for God.

Prayer
Lord, come to my help. Amen.

"The hungry he has filled with good things."
(Luke 1:53)

December

22

Background
One of the great rules of salvation history is expressed here, namely that one must be in need to be saved; one must be hungry in order to be filled with good things. We find this in God's feeding of the people of Israel during their forty years in the wilderness (see Exodus 16:4-35). We find it again when God's angel brought food to Daniel in the lion's den (see Daniel 14:31-40) and to Elijah under the broom tree in the desert (see 1 Kings 19:5-8).

Reflection
As we enter the final days before Christmas, we may find that most of our time and energy are caught up in the whirlwind of shopping, decorating, cooking, etc. We may even begin to wonder if we have lost sight of what it is all about. Within the hurly-burly, we must never forget that we are perpetuating the spirit that caused the first Christmas: the gift of Jesus to us!

To Think About
What do I really want for Christmas?

Prayer
Lord, even though I may not think of you often this day, please don't forget me. Amen.

December

23

Her neighbors and relatives heard that the Lord had shown his great mercy toward her, and they rejoiced with her. (Luke 1:58)

Background

At the time of Jesus, women in Palestine are not accorded as much status as men. The birth of a boy is a source of great joy. There is even a saying: "The birth of a male child causes universal joy, but the birth of a female child causes universal sorrow." Not only does Elizabeth give birth at a time when child-bearing seems impossible for her, but the child born is a male—both reasons for great jubilation.

Reflection

While it can be relatively easy to grieve with others, it is often difficult to truly rejoice with them. Because we are human, envy is never far from us. What we fail to appreciate is that when God blesses someone, that blessing is given to be shared. By right, the blessings of one belong to all. Mary's blessing is not just hers; rather, it is a blessing that is to be shared by all throughout eternity.

To Think About

The one who has nothing to share is the poorest of all.

Prayer

May I never stop counting my blessings. Amen.

" . . . for you will go before the Lord to prepare his ways." (Luke 1:76)

Background
The Jews are hoping for the coming of the anointed king, the Messiah, and they believe that a forerunner will announce his arrival. It is generally believed that this person will be Elijah (see Malachi 4:5). To this day, the Jews set a place at table for Elijah when they celebrate their Passover meal.

Reflection
We are told that each one of us adds a page to the gospel every day by the deeds we do and the things we say. Our mission is to bring good news to others. Like Mary, we are called to allow the mystery of Christmas to continue every day. If people are to receive the gift of Jesus, it will be through you and me, through his love that they experience from us.

To Think About
The greatest gift that I can give another this Christmas is the gift of Jesus Christ.

Prayer
Spirit of the living God, fall afresh on me. Amen.

December

25

But to those who did accept him he gave power to become children of God. (John 1:12)

Background

How people become God's children through acceptance of Jesus is the theme of the second half of John's Gospel. By accepting Jesus, the human is adopted into the life of the Trinity. Saint Athanasius tells us: "The Son of God became man in order that the sons of men, the sons of Adam, might become sons of God. He is the Son of God by nature; we, by grace."

Reflection

Cecil B. de Mille reckoned that over eight million people saw his silent movie *King of Kings.* When asked why he didn't remake it later using sound, he replied: "If Jesus spoke with a southern accent then the people of the north would not accept him and vice versa. As it is everyone accepts him." Today we celebrate the simple fact that God is with us. We can lay our troubles aside and rejoice.

To Think About

Others may know that it is Christmas only by the warmth of my welcome.

Prayer

Lord, be my companion along the road of life. Amen.

"You will be hated by all because of my name, but whoever endures to the end will be saved."
(Matthew 10:22)

Background

When Jesus invites people to follow him, he does not promise them an easy life; rather, he promises them a life marked by persecution. This persecution will come from the state, the Church, and even one's families. However, Jesus also promises that anyone who withstands this persecution will have the promise of eternal life.

Reflection

Christianity is a call given each day, a summons to live according to the gospel. This will often necessitate making unpopular decisions that may cause us to be excluded from popular circles. Ultimately, it is the crucified Christ who beckons and it is to him we must answer. His call will always involve a carrying of the cross as it is presented to us in our lives.

To Think About

To thine own self be true. (W. Shakespeare)

Prayer

Into thy hands I commend my spirit. Amen.

December

26

December

27

. . . he saw and he believed. (John 20:8)

Background

Saint Thomas Aquinas tells us: "The individual arguments taken alone are not sufficient proof of Christ's resurrection, but taken together in a cumulative way, they manifest it perfectly." While the empty tomb and other facts point to the resurrection of Jesus, acceptance of Jesus' resurrection demands individual faith. Even though Mary of Magdala tells the disciples that Jesus is risen, they have to experience this for themselves.

Reflection

A woman had her elderly father, who had Parkinson's disease, move in with her and her family. Because the man spilled his food and broke the dishware, his daughter put him at a separate table at mealtime and gave him wooden utensils to use. When he died, his daughter threw out the wooden plates and bowls, but was surprised to see her five-year-old daughter rescuing them. "I need to keep them for when you get old, Mother!" the young girl explained.

To Think About

While others may not practice what I preach, they will often imitate what I do.

Prayer

May I be your beacon for others. Amen.

. . . they found him in the temple. . . . (Luke 2:46)

Background
When a Jewish boy reaches the age of twelve, he becomes a "son of the law" and is obliged to live by the law. For Jesus, this includes attendance at his first Passover at the tender age of twelve. He is, no doubt, fascinated by the life about the Temple, especially the custom whereby the Sanhedrin meet in the Temple court to discuss theological and legal questions for all who care to listen.

Reflection
Some people cannot experience Jesus in the temple, the church, or the chapel. Perhaps they have not first found him in the temple, church, or chapel of their hearts. Unless we put some preparation into it, going to church will often prove to be an empty experience for us. As with anything in life, we can only hope to reap what we sow. The result will often be determined by the effort that has been made.

To Think About
Can I hope to find God on a Sunday if I haven't found him on the other six days of the week?

Prayer
Lord, may we always be for each other. Amen.

December

29

"Now, Master, you may let your servant go in peace . . . for my eyes have seen your salvation."
(Luke 2:29-30)

Background
Simon's canticle, which is often called the Nunc Dimittis, can be divided into two sections. The first is an act of thanksgiving to God for having sent the long-awaited Messiah. The second is a prophecy foretelling the blessings that will come with the Messiah, especially the salvation that will be for all.

Reflection
It has been said that life can be seen either as a mystery to be lived or a problem to be solved. If we see salvation as an ongoing event, something that is interwoven in each and every event of our lives, then all of life becomes an unfolding of a plan of love. Everything that happens is seen to be working for our good, even if we cannot see it at the time.

To Think About
Life is penetrated with all that is sacred.

Prayer
Lord, open my eyes to the beauty of your love.
Amen.

She never left the temple, but worshipped night and day with fasting and prayer. (Luke 2:37)

Background
Like all the great people of the Bible, Anna never loses touch with the one who is the source of her strength and hope. She does this by means of her private prayer and fasting. By means of these two gifts, she is able to become completely open to God and can dispose herself to doing whatever God asks.

Reflection
Fasting has not enjoyed popular press in recent years. While it is not an end in itself, it does have a place in any spirit-filled life. When we fast, we are in fact saying to God: "I am trusting you for the very sustenance that I need for my body." In this way, fasting becomes a prayer that is experienced at the root of our being. Saint Benedict taught that "to work is to pray"; in a similar way, to fast is to pray.

To Think About
The absence of food can become food for prayer.

Prayer
May my hunger be transformed into a hunger for you. Amen.

December

31

All things came to be through him, and without him nothing came to be. (John 1:3)

Background

Professor John Paterson gives us an insight into the power that a word had in the Hebrew mind. He says: "The spoken word to the Hebrew was fearfully alive ... It was a unit of energy charged with power. It flies like a bullet to its billet." We find this in many places in the Old Testament: in Isaiah 55:10-11, for example, where the word of God is portrayed as being something that has a creative power.

Reflection

There's a little saying that goes: "Get down on your knees and thank God you're on your feet." This is just another way of saying that we should be eternally grateful for all the gifts we enjoy yet so often take for granted. Everything we have is a gift from God given to us through Jesus Christ. What more beautiful way to begin a new year than by consecrating all that we have to Jesus!

To Think About

Freely I have received, freely I give.

Prayer

Lord, I return to you all that you have so generously given to me. Amen.

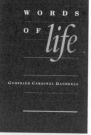